THE BACK HOME SERIES

SERIES TITLES

At the Lake
Jim Landwehr

Body Talk
Takwa Gordon

The In-Between State
Martha Lundin

North Freedom
Carolyn Dallmann

Ohio Apertures
Robert Miltner

"In these big hearted and quietly humorous essays, Scott Morris reveals a world studded by a thousand possible points of contact—be they via books or pie-making, faith or furry rodents. As our guide through that world, Morris is a veteran essayist, writing with enough distance to take stock of his own life, but with the courage and curiosity needed to take stock, too, of that distance and ask why and how it exists. This book is a gift."

—SARAH VIREN
author of *To Name the Bigger Lie*

"My high school physics teacher warned the class, in no uncertain words, not to touch the brooding electric analog calculator in the back of the room, and, whatever you do, never ever divide by zero. Of course, we did do that the first time we were left alone with it. Reading Scott Russell Morris's elegant essays in *Points of Tangency*—insightful glances of this this and that that, spanning a whole protractor of angles of attack—reminded me of that ancient engine and how it sputtered and whirred, its gears searching ceaselessly for the infinity of solutions, its gears meshing and missing, thinking it could divide any and every number by nothing. To essay, Morris reminds us (as he is very good at placing precise pressure on a single word) means to attempt, but I tend to think (dividing any number by nothing) more and more that these "essays" are more like "worries." I worried the notion of worrying as I read this prose rosary, this secular chaplet, amazed by Morris's prowess to manipulate the multitude of points he held in his hand. *Komboloi*! Each essay is a key on a ring of keys that opens everything or nothing or *Nothing*. Like poetry, nothing happens here, like a dog worrying a bone into a banquet or a squirrel worrying an acorn into an oak tree.

—MICHAEL MARTONE
author of *Plain Air: Sketches from Winesburg, Indiana*

"Scott Russell Morris knows that the mind, at its most inspired, its most insightful, doesn't follow a predictable train of thought. It swerves, sprints ahead, doubles back, burrows down, climbs up, leaps, plummets, crashes, then shakes itself out again. It's a squirrel, endlessly finding the nut it forgot it buried. Morris's essays move the way our innermost thoughts do, with a catchy sense of discovery, recovery, and delight."

—ERIC LEMAY
author of *Remember Me*

"In *Points of Tangency*, Morris captures a true sense of personal intimacy—and by intimacy, I mean the kind you would expect from a long, late-night conversation with friends, the ones that give you the courage to go back and face the world. Perhaps it is his genius for living in a question, refusing to close it with an answer, or his willingness to trust that the reader will take his vulnerability as an invitation and not a confession, or maybe even his gift for following his own musings 'until you see them in the mystery of their own specificity,' yet in any case, Morris' themes remain fresh and relevant and deeply resonant throughout. His deft exploration of what it means to touch another human life, to lose and to find and to struggle with what we have, and how we mind the gaps and write new words to the poem possesses all the hallmarks we crave in a satisfying read: wit, generosity, and above all, a unique insight into what it means to be human."

—MICAH MULDOWNEY
author of *Q-Drive and Other Poems*

POINTS
OF
TANGENCY

Essays

SCOTT RUSSELL MORRIS

CORNERSTONE PRESS
UNIVERSITY OF WISCONSIN-STEVENS POINT

Cornerstone Press, Stevens Point, Wisconsin 54481
Copyright © 2024 Scott Russell Morris
www.uwsp.edu/cornerstone

Printed in the United States of America by
Point Print and Design Studio, Stevens Point, Wisconsin

Library of Congress Control Number: 2024940426
ISBN: 978-1-960329-50-9

Cover art: "Daniel Crommelin Verplanck," John Singleton Copley, 1771.

This is a work of nonfiction. All of the events in this book are true to the best of
the author's memory. Some names and identifying features have been changed to
protect the identity of certain parties. The author in no way represents any company,
corporation, or brand, mentioned herein. The views expressed in this memoir are
solely those of the author.

Cornerstone Press titles are produced in courses and internships offered by the
Department of English at the University of Wisconsin–Stevens Point.

DIRECTOR & PUBLISHER
Dr. Ross K. Tangedal

EXECUTIVE EDITORS
Jeff Snowbarger, Freesia McKee

EDITORIAL DIRECTOR
Ellie Atkinson

SENIOR EDITORS
Brett Hill, Grace Dahl

PRESS STAFF
Chloe Cieszynski, Allison Lange, Sophie McPherson, Eva Nielsen, Ava Willett

For Kirsten

ESSAYS

NOTHING IN PARTICULAR

I sit to write and nothing comes to mind…
…which is as good a topic as any, so let's begin:

Nothing is a hopeless word. My high school teachers emphasized, over and over, that *thing* is unacceptable in a paper, so *nothing* must be a double no-no. The word tells your readers nothing. "Be specific," the teachers advised. I now give the same advice to my own students. If you mean peach, say *peach*. If you mean Eurasian red squirrel, say *Eurasian red squirrel*. To say "Nothing comes to mind," is a lie, of course. As I sit here typing, trying to work out an essay with an infinite stretch of white below the cursor, my thoughts aren't connected. Perhaps that lack of connections is the nothingness weighing down on me, perhaps my mind's wanderings—a snowed-in weekend, an unanswered prayer, and that moment just after you finish a book—are the stars adrift in that void, moving with an unseen but no less certain trajectory.

COMMON PHRASEOLOGY HAS US SAYING, "In the beginning was the void," or "In the beginning there was nothing." But that isn't true. Genesis says, "In the beginning God created the heaven and the earth." So, there was God, and immediately a place for him to live and a place for us. Even secular thought says that there was something there; the Big Bang was an explosion of condensed matter. It may have been the only speck of matter in all of existence, but it was there tainting the nothingness of space with its inherent somethingness. Which was superior, space or that condensed matter? Was the Nothing ruined by the Something, or the Something surrounded by the Nothing?

MY SOPHOMORE YEAR OF COLLEGE, over Presidents' Day Weekend, some friends and I visited my roommate Tim's grandparents' farm in Ashton, Idaho. It had been snowing since we arrived late Friday night, but it was coming down particularly hard on Sunday. When we emptied out of the church building, the car had already accumulated three or four inches of snow. The flakes fell like tufts of tissue paper and were only getting bigger. We drove back to the farmhouse, Tim steering the car with white knuckles and slow, deliberate movements. We drove through the white void. From the back passenger window, I took a picture of the landscape: the photograph shows a blank, vaguely blue convergence of sky and ground and the flurrying flakes reflecting the flash give the only shape to the nothingness of the horizon. We arrived safe, though, because we discovered the road was marked on both sides by small stakes with orange flags of tape which the snow had not quite covered. We saw the stakes enter our vision one at a time, and we trained our eyes on each as they came and went.

Later that evening, Tim's grandparents, aunt, and uncle decided to visit a neighbor.

"If we're not back by 6:30, call the sheriff," Tim's grandfather said, only partially in jest. Around 6:45 we got a call from the neighbor saying they should have been home by now. They did not answer their cell phone. Tim said they knew how to handle the weather, he was sure they

were fine. Around 7:30, when we were actually thinking about calling the sheriff, they finally called us. They'd
gotten stuck in the snow not far away: could Tim drive the
truck out to them? Tim, Jessie, and Andy, natives to the
cold and smart enough to bring appropriate clothes for a
winter trip, put on their gear and charged into negative
20 degrees. I had nothing to offer, except that I lent Andy
my gloves—the only warm items I brought—because in
his haste he couldn't find his. I watched as they readied
the truck, and then, when that also proved to be stuck,
they resorted to the tractor with the snow blower attached.
Alone in a stranger's house while everyone else thought
of practical things to do, I watched. I tried to justify: I
am a Southern California boy, used to paradisaical San
Diego weather, not Idaho blizzards. But surely there was
something I could have done, had I more street smarts
or even just direction. It didn't help that earlier in the
day Tim's grandfather had mentioned that all ten of his
children were raised on the farm, and they knew how to
work. My dad taught me to *work*, I had thought in reply. I
helped him file documents, keep accounts, assemble mass
mailings. I sometimes proofread emails to his clients. And
my mom had been an artist, specializing in Christmas
décor, and when she'd had her workstation set out on the
kitchen table, readying for the craft fairs that earned her
enough money to pay for Christmases each year, she had
let me hot glue pompoms to glass ornaments.

Eventually, I got up the courage to help and put on the
coat I'd brought—a nice brown leather thing, perfect for
those bone-chilling 57-degree San Diego nights—and my
tennis shoes. I started walking toward the snow blower

when Andy came up the snow-covered driveway and told me to go back inside.

"There's nothing you can do," he said and handed back my gloves. "I was just standing there myself." So we both went in, and the family abandoned the cars on the road and trudged through the snow to stand by the farmhouse fire. We all had hot chocolate and wassail to celebrate their safe return.

A NOUN, AS THE COLLOQUIAL definition goes, is a person, place, or thing. *Nothing* certainly is neither a person nor a place. It definitely and definitively is not a thing, except, of course, grammatically.

"There is nothing here," we might say as casually as we say, "There are squirrels in that tree." But *is* equals existence. *Nothing* is zip, zilch, nil, null, zero, empty. And yet "There is nothing" still makes sense. Poets and neuro-linguists love such ambiguities. I love such ambiguities, though I wouldn't consider myself a poet and I am terrible at all forms of neurology.

ABSOLUTE ZERO IS THE THEORETICAL POINT at which all energy is gone from a system and no matter is moving, the coldest possible temperature. It may not exist, but it has been given a name anyhow so that when it is discovered we will already have a neat, tidy place for it in our catalog of the universe's mysteries. Space closely approaches absolute zero at about 4°K, with the Boomerang Nebula being the coldest known place in the universe at a record 1°K. Almost nothing, but not quite—an honorable mention for the attempt though.

Vacuum also draws images of nothingness. The ideal vacuum means nothingness, but real-world vacuums aren't nothing, they are just less. Significantly less pressure, less matter. Space is also called a vacuum, suggesting that it is emptiness, but who can look at the stars and say that there is nothing in space? Perhaps the stars are farther apart than we are able to contemplate, but how close do objects have to be before the space between stops having nothing and suddenly contains both objects? And who are we to determine such distances?

"MOM, THERE'S NOTHING TO EAT," I said on countless afternoons of my youth.

"Have an apple."

"There's nothing on TV."

"Read a book."

"I have nothing to write about."

I FEEL LIKE I SHOULD MENTION, before I ramble too far, that there is a difference between "nothing to do" and "boredom." Personally, I am rather fond of having nothing to do. I think all too frequently people have far too much to do. Robert Louis Stevenson perhaps says it best: "Extreme *busyness*, whether at school or college, kirk or market, is a symptom of deficient vitality; and a faculty for idleness implies a catholic appetite and a strong sense of personal identity." To idle, to do nothing, is the only way to really live, to live for yourself and no one else.

Having internalized this line of thinking as a child, I often laid around the house on the most comfortable couch, the yellow and blue checked one in the den. When the book I was reading, either finished or grown dull, dropped to the floor, I just stared at the ceiling. If my mom saw me in such a state of reverie, she would say, "If you're bored, I can find something for you to do."

"I'm not bored," was always my response. *Something* meant chores. Nothing beat something every time, like rocks to scissors. My mother, for her part, seemed to accept that answer as satisfactory. She was herself an accomplished idler, as all creative types must be. Seeing her spend her day on the couch with a novel gave me permission to do the same. In fact, the novels she left on the coffee table often found their way into my own room. It was in this way that I first read *The Left Hand of Darkness* and *Fahrenheit 451*.

My father, a businessman, didn't bother asking if I was bored. Seeing me laying on the couch—even if I *was* reading—he would ask if I'd prayed yet that day, or studied the scriptures, if I'd done my homework, if my room was clean. Always straight to the point, boredom having nothing to do with what was good and needful, the practical facts of spiritual and domestic work. If the answer to all those was "yes" he would then ask if I'd read anything nonfiction lately. An idea I scoffed at, bound as I was to science fiction and fantasy.

BECAUSE *NOTHING* IS ONLY A WORD, just a concept, it becomes a placeholder, and recognizing that, I am forced to emphasize that something does exist where nothing is evident.

AS MY FATHER WANTED, I did study the scriptures, and I did so with the zeal of an obsessive overachiever. Having read *Jurassic Park* in just two weeks the summer before fourth grade, I set my sights high and decided I would read the entirety of the scriptures that year, starting with the Bible. I did not make it past Numbers (a shame, I now know, since Judges is where the Old Testament really gets interesting.) But I did read the Book of Mormon, fueled by my father's intense faith in it. I was struck most of all by the first story, about a prophet named Lehi and his son, Nephi. When Lehi has a vision of the Tree of Life, Nephi desires the same vision and prays to receive it. God does not just grant his prayer but sends an angel to explain the vision's rich, complicated symbolism.

I wanted the same thing. And, to be specific, by *thing* I mean I wanted visions. I wanted a God of Angels and Answers. I wanted to make good on the promise that nothing would be withheld to those with a desire to believe. I wanted the knowledge of the universe poured into my mind while I slept. I wanted to wake afire.

I spent many dark nights of my childhood on my knees, seeking what the prophets saw, certain that receiving a vision would be to know something for certain.

SOCIETY, FOR THE MOST PART, favors my father's business-like, to-the-point view of things, though perhaps not so spiritually bent. My father, a salesman for publishing houses for much of his career and married to a reader and writer of children's poems, wasn't so adamantly against reading or other nothings, but he was ever concerned with the practical. When I announced that I would do my MFA in creative writing, he asked if perhaps that would lead to a career in law. It is this love affair with practicality, with busyness, that I suppose I am hesitant to embrace, despite its virtues.

For example, you run into an old friend you haven't seen in a while. After the normal pleasantries, they ask:

"So, what are you doing these days?"

"Nothing much," you reply (or at least, this is how I reply). You (I) politely ask what they are up to lately.

"I am so busy…" and then they list the societies they belong to, the home and family improvement projects, the calendars they are juggling, their job, their classes, their dog, and onward. Who wins the conversation? All judges point to the busy one. By listing their activities, they are value signaling, showing that they are engaged with the world, that they are selfless, that they have a self who is important to other people and their dog. I have all these same things to do, too, of course (except the dog—reader, I am a cat person), but in my own virtue-signaling I tend to ignore all that. Perhaps it's just a reluctance to believe the mundanities of my life are at all interesting to other people, but partially it is because I value the selfish side of myself, the one that carves out time for just me. I am not the first of my generation who would be called self-indulgent in this way, taking advantage of privileges we too infrequently examine, but we are following the natural progression of societies: after the affluence comes the generation of dreamers and artists.

Also, obviously, I don't really do "nothing" all day. Teaching is something, and the way I earn money. Walking is something: relaxation and exercise. Doing the laundry and cleaning the bathroom, it turns out, are very essential somethings. There's a lot of paperwork involved in doing anything, even nothing, if you want an apartment to do it in. Writing essays is certainly something, even if a lot of that something is actually just gleaning Wikipedia for fun facts about squirrels.

AND SOMETIMES READING IS NOTHING, but sometimes it's also everything. I was in eighth grade and had just read Lois Lowry's *The Giver*. I was lying on that same yellow and blue check couch in the den, where the light was always faintly golden and hazy, easing the drift into sleep. *The Giver*'s ending baffled me; I was mad and delighted at the same time. I see now that I had a little bit of a reader's crush on Jonas, the main character. I was also jealous of his power to receive and conjure visions. When I finished the novel, with its warm, snowy ending, I put the book down and stared at the bearded old man on the cover, and then at the ceiling, and then back at the book.

The way I thought about literature changed in that moment. Though I was already someone who read all the time, this was my first glimpse at how necessary reading is for a soul to speak to another soul. The best literature, I was beginning to feel, was about both loss and love at the same time, about the sacrifices necessary to keep one's convictions. And this, too, was my first delight in literary ambiguity, not knowing what to think of that last beautiful scene in the book: so much snow, all you could think about was snow, and Jonas is stumbling with the baby through the deep snow, and there in the distance, people singing around a warm hearth. Was this Jonas's last memory to give? Was this death? Was this a happy ending? For her part, Lowry has said she never intended the ending to be ambiguous, had always intended for a happy ending, but this is neither here nor there. What is important is that staring into nothing, contemplating the expanse of popcorn ceiling above me, was the only way to examine the new shape of my soul.

[This page intentionally left blank]

ZERO MAY BE NOTHING, but we attach to it so much emotional weight. The glass half-full/half-empty debate is really a way of asking if we see something or nothing when we have the choice between the two.

We abhor zero the way nature abhors a vacuum. Just think back to high school math, when after doing all that work, canceling out y and multiplying dividends or whatever (can you tell I lost interest in math somewhere along the way?) the answer was x = 0. So frustrating, all that work for nothing.

THE THEORY OF ABIOGENESIS, now commonly called *spontaneous generation*, was a scientific misconception that held sway from at least the time of Aristotle until the 1700s. Spontaneous generation holds that some complicated organic life forms are generated by the decomposition of other organic matter. Aristotle noted that aphids were born of dew; maggots generated by rotting meat; mice created from old hay; and crocodiles spawned by fallen logs in swamps. Essentially, it was a something from nothing approach to life.

When the first scientists began challenging these "vulgar errors," others lashed back. "To question [spontaneous generation] is to question reason," Alexander Ross wrote. The textbook experiment shows a flask with meat in it. When the flask is left uncovered, maggots appear on the meat. When the flask is covered completely, nothing happens. When the flask is covered with a semi-permeable covering, maggots appear on top of the covering but not on the bait. Through these means Francesco Redi determined that maggots did not come from rotting meat, but rather

omne vivum ex ovo
[Every living thing from an egg.]

An egg, but not a goose egg, except for goslings. Or, as Rodgers and Hammerstein lyricized:

Nothing comes from nothing,
Nothing ever could.

THE FIRST TIME I PRAYED, I mean really prayed, prayed with tears coming down my cheeks, prayed with the scriptures open, with my mouth open, actually saying the words, pleading to know if God was real, I was sitting in the fire escape of my freshman dorms, next to the door to the roof, where I knew no one would be. I would have gone to the roof itself, but that required a special key, so I sat uncomfortably on the dusty steps, as high as I could get. I must have spent at least an hour up there asking God if I'd successfully masked the queer parts of myself I wanted so much to be rid of. The steps chilled my body, the roof's door remained locked above me.

But nothing. Just a tightening in my chest and in my throat, salt on my cheeks. I was asking if I should continue in the church, if there was forgiveness for lusting after men, if all this work to be good was worth it. I no longer expected angels or visions, but I still believed in answers, and yet, nothing. Nothing at all.

My body and my convictions shook. Without a knowledge or a personal witness, I came down off the stairs.

Faith was moving forward with nothing else.

IN THE TAROT DECK, the 0 card is the Fool.

Biddy Tarot (my go-to tarot website) says 0 is "the number of unlimited potential," but also notes that because the deck represents the Fool's journey, "he is ever present and therefore needs no number." He is at once unnumbered and yet any of the numbers, because when we look at the other cards, we must remember that we're seeing the Fool, a reflection of ourselves, just a person on a journey who is, at his core, only himself, nothing more. The Fool is the cosmic adventurer, the perfect anthropomorphizing of existentialism, a symbol that the querent needs to (or at least, can) remove everything else from himself and start at the beginning again, to look at himself from his very core, with nothing else to distract him.

I LIKE THAT *ZERO* IS THE SHAPE IT IS. 0. Just a line circumnavigating nothing, as though by encircling a void in a line of something, anything, we might understand it or keep it close by. We know exactly what isn't there in the center, giving us something to work with. The early Babylonians had no notion of *nothing*. They left a blank space where we now put a zero, nothing to represent nothing. Even their blank space is still a symbol of sorts, an absence that speaks, or perhaps tells its story through its silence, the way children often do when accused of mischief, but that isn't good enough for modern thinkers. We want unfathomable depths condensed to symbols. We want more zeros on the end of our paychecks.

Nothing is just an idea. Which means it doesn't exist, or rather exists only in our heads and on paper so that we have a notion of it, because in minds and on paper all words are things, representations of ever-entangled ideas, ideas more complex than even dictionaries can convey.

These little nothings—sweet nothings, like a lover's whispers—form our world, or our view of it, and so we form ourselves from nothing in particular.

AS A MORMON MISSIONARY, I was allowed next to nothing of the outside world. We were asked to forsake all things: no books except the scriptures and a few selected texts by modern church leaders. No TV, no radio, no newspapers. No contact with home except weekly, hand-written letters. And no privacy, either, as missionaries are assigned a 24/7 companion who becomes your co-worker, roommate, and constant friend. My first companion was the sincerest of people, a down-home sort of fellow from the Pacific Northwest, a white man raised on a First Nations reservation. He was nothing like I: he admitted to me that until getting an audio version of the Book of Mormon a few months prior, he had never read a book cover to cover (a result of dyslexia, not entirely his own choice.) He was a champion boxer, accustomed to using his body to break people and fix things. He was not zealous, but his quiet faith seemed entirely unshakable. I secretly believed he resented my distaste for cycling, but he didn't complain as we walked from appointment to appointment. For all this, I liked him immensely. I had the uncharacteristically good sense to check my grammar-correcting impulse, but felt there was little to talk about otherwise.

Which is all to say, that in the first few months as a missionary, I felt adrift from myself. Not a bad thing, but I was looking for something, anything, to be my own when none of the things that were *me* were allowed. I was not the only one who felt this way, we were a world of self-policing nineteen-year-olds trying hard to be earnest, and everyone had a thing. Many elders collected colorful ties, one marked on his area map the location of every 7-11 and became a Big Gulp connoisseur. Another elder I knew perfected the virgin margarita, which bordered on sacrilegious given the no-alcohol, no-partying rules, but secretly, we all loved his dollar-store mixer. My thing was squirrels.

I had, of course, seen squirrels before, but not in such abundance as they are to be found in the DC area. For some reason, as my companion and I biked through a run-down Maryland suburb filled with unmown lawns and dim ramblers, I noticed a squirrel circle her way around the trunk of a wide-canopied magnolia tree just as we rolled down a hill and sharply turned a corner. I kept my eyes on her and let the momentum carry me. Perhaps it was the way her tail spiraled and disappeared, reappearing again on the ground, but the moment of sciurus grace caught my attention.

Then, a few days later, walking through the exact same neighborhood, the same street but farther down, just before the road met the path that led through the woods to the park, I heard a noise overhead and looked up, almost in the same manner as when I'd prayed, almost like finishing a book and seeing myself for the first time in a cold world. The sky was overcast and pale, the trees reached high into the sky and across the road toward each other, their branches bare in mid-autumn observance, and leaping through the distance from one exposed twig to another, a squirrel. I could not see her color, silhouetted as she was against the white sky, but I was enraptured. *Enthused*, in its original etymology, suggests being possessed by a god, engulfed in the spirit. I was, from that moment on, a squirrel enthusiast.

Was this the answer I had wanted? It is silly to suggest such a thing, but there was a miracle happening, even if it was not a vision. If I sound like I am being overly dramatic about it all, then you'll understand my predicament. It was nothing. Really, nothing. Well, it wasn't nothing, it was a squirrel, but the quotidian nature of squirrels, their smallness, my own obsessiveness, was everything. To me, the squirrel leaping above was permission, whether divine or self-indulgent, to see into the nothingness, to examine it, to embrace it.

THE FIRST TIME I WROTE A personal essay, in an introduction to creative writing course, I was again on a weekend away with friends, again in Idaho, this time at a different roommate's parents' house in Eagleton. My friends relaxed by the pool, no snow this time, and while they partied, I was inside typing away because I had procrastinated finishing my homework. At some point, I realized that although I had a lot more to say on the nature of friendship at first sight, I also wanted to go swimming and to be close to a girl I was too nervous to flirt with. New to the form, I didn't know how to end the essay, so I made a decision that went against my obsessive, do-gooder, straight-A sensibilities: I simply stopped typing and submitted the essay unfinished.

My professor said he loved the ending and I knew I had found a calling.

And in that spirit, I leave you, not with nothing left to write, but having already said nothing at all.

ON WHOM THINGS ARE LOST

Try to be one of the people on whom nothing is lost.

—Henry James

I am not one of *those* people. Things are lost on me, and by me, all the time.

FOR EXAMPLE, I LOST THE FIRST draft of this essay. No joke. Given the theme of this essay, I am pleased that it worked out this way; it's perfect, really, that I should lose an essay about losing things.

I started the essay in March and had written a fairly thorough draft, probably eight or nine pages. It was a rough draft, to be sure, but I was pleased with where it was going. As is my general habit, I didn't touch the essay for several weeks. When I tried to come back to the essay in early June, I couldn't find it anywhere. I checked every folder on my computer, twice, including the recycle bin. I searched for the word "lost" with the computer's search feature (in the process discovering the manuscript of an award-winning ghost story I'd written as an undergraduate, which I thought I'd accidentally deleted years ago, which has the phrase "lost at sea" in its critical moment). I checked and double-checked my portable hard drive and both of my flash drives; I checked my laptop; I checked my work laptop; I checked my email to see if I had sent it to myself. I couldn't find it anywhere. Gone.

I spent hours smoldering quietly and rummaging through the electronic sinkhole that my computer had apparently become before I gave up the search and restarted from scratch. I felt the loss of that first essay keenly, though it was a delectably laughable loss. With any other essay, I might have just given up, but after the initial frustration, I got back to work, now with both less and more material.

And yet, this is not the same essay it would have been; I've forgotten the witty way I alluded to the TV show *Lost* without actually mentioning it; the connection between salt which has lost its savor and books that I can't find. I remember these cultural references, but I can't for the life of me remember the language I'd used to incorporate them, or why I thought they were necessary. On top of all that, I am not the same person I was then either. When I started that first draft in March, I couldn't know that in August, just a few weeks after starting the second first draft, mere days after the story at the center of this essay, I would meet the woman I would marry, which isn't what this essay is about, but colors the musings so that my selves are woven together, written over each other, a palimpsest of personas.

DAVID SHIELDS QUOTES Patrick Duff to tell us:

> *All memories are predicated on loss. . . It's through the act of remembering that we bring these forgotten experiences back from oblivion. . . Our memories are filled with gaps and distortions, because by its very nature memory is selective.*

The act of writing and recording those memories is equally selective and equally distorting. In writing these stories down, I reshape them yet again. But here goes:

When I was young, my family twice stopped at Zion National Park and hiked a trail called the Narrows, which follows a series of shallow side-winding twists in the placid Virgin River as it creates a beautiful chasm of high canyon walls with sandy beaches and smooth stones. I remember water snakes gliding along the sunny surface; I remember areas I was frightened to step in because the water reached my thighs; I remember a particular bend in the river where the sandbar was widest, where a single tree clutched a shadowed cliff and jettisoned itself into the sunlight. In that bend, where the water was deepest, my older, more adventurous brother Michael took off his shirt and dove from the canyon wall into the pool. I remember this spot in particular because on both occasions I tried to swim with my brother and lost a shoe. I remember peeling off my shoes while I still stood ankle deep in water, feeling how the gentle river tugged the shoes from my fingers; I remember the way my mom tried not to laugh and the way my dad's eyes flickered when he learned my shoe was gone.

I'VE LOST SLEEP; CONFIDENCE in myself; the cap for several of my camera lenses; time; my mother and all of my grand-parents; car keys, house keys, work keys, bike-lock keys, pretty much any key ever given me; computer passwords; the remote shutter control for my camera only two weeks after receiving it for Christmas; the replacement remote shutter control I then purchased for myself because I didn't want to lose face with the gift giver; books; money, both literally and figuratively; games; weight; opportunities;

a yellow tie with a blue-checked pattern; my flash drive; my train of thought.

HERE IS ANOTHER STORY, which was true enough when I first wrote it, but its truths have been lost to time:

The same week I began writing this essay for the second time, a friend told me she loved me. In fact, she said "no other girl in the world" loved me the way she does. Which, as far as I could tell, was probably true, but I had no feelings for her. We were friends, and I welcomed the friendship, but that was all.

"Why don't you love me?" she asked. "Is it because I'm not smart enough?"

What is a man to do when a woman calls him Prince Charming and pours her heart out to him, but there is nothing in his heart to return to her? Her intellect is actually quite impressive. And she always gave me perfect, handmade gifts, like a camera bag with a squirrel patch, a squirrel collage, and a painting of a squirrel at Delicate Arch. I lied: "There's nothing in particular."

There were in fact some rather particular things: the way she sometimes talked down to my socially awkward younger brother, with whom I shared an apartment; the way every little drama sent her into a flurry of emotion; the way she didn't talk to me for three months when she found out I had asked an old friend whom I hadn't seen in almost a year for a date; the way she frequently asked if I was mad at her though I never was. But I wasn't about to expound on what I thought her faults were. I rationalized that I would have told her these things specifically if we had been dating, as though to be a couple were the demarcating line of emotional honesty, the time when such a discussion might have been appropriate. She had confronted me while I was in the street, walking away from my duplex while she had been walking toward it. Standing in the open, next to an empty lot, I felt exposed, pressured. I didn't want to tell her how I felt, but I especially didn't want her to know that even though she, my brother, and I had made plans for the evening, I was actually bailing to go on a date. I had tried to leave early so as not to cross paths with her. I tried to change the subject and acted like I didn't notice how much she was hurting, like I couldn't see what the conversation cost her.

Besides, I would tell myself later, those things I didn't like weren't important for our friendship. I liked having her as a friend. But I confess that I was not always as good a friend to her as I could have been. I kept hoping that she would become less interested—there were times when I intentionally didn't laugh at her jokes; didn't smile too big when I saw her; evaded those good-bye hugs that are commonplace in my other friendships; avoided sitting next to her in public; occasionally didn't invite her to outings with other friends; made sure to talk about her in a way that people would know we were just friends, especially when I was otherwise complimenting her and giving her the high praise she deserved: all this as a way of hoping she would get the hint. I feel a deep sense of guilt for treating her badly, but especially for not treating her well.

What bothers me is what I lost in turning her down, not a romantic relationship, but a more meaningful connection to a friend. I was aloof, cold. We were still friends, but no longer as close as we could have been. She no longer laughed so much at my jokes; she didn't smile so big when she saw me; she no longer requested good-bye hugs, though she still gave them to my younger brother; she made no special effort to sit near me in public; she didn't invite me as often to outings with friends; she still talked about me but only in the casual way a friend mentions another friend. Sure, she had gotten the hint, but what did I gain from my callousness?

THE SECOND FIRST DRAFT OF THIS ESSAY, when I sat down to rewrite the written pages but instead began to write about my friend's broken heart, was not written in Wordsworthian tranquility. It was written after guilt had persistently bothered me for several days. But when I returned to the essay again, months later, that guilt, though not gone, was dulled. The parts I wrote as a "spontaneous overflow" and the ones I recall "in tranquility" are at differences now, but both truths resound in their time, even if neither tells the complete story.

"WHY DON'T YOU LOVE ME?"

She was not the first to try to get through to me. In high school, I went on casual dates, but never had a girlfriend or boyfriend, though several girls and one boy unsuccessfully expressed their interests, only to be turned down. Reader, don't get me wrong: I was neither popular nor a player, but I was friendly, enthusiastic, and quirky enough to be intriguing to a certain nerdy subset of the high school population. I told my enthusiasts, rather too harshly sometimes, that I couldn't date them because we didn't share the same religious values, but this was a lie. I didn't pursue any of the Mormon girls either. I was more interested in books and solitude and myself than people. I had learned to fear my own sexuality, but also my favorite song was

Simon and Garfunkel's *I Am a Rock*: "I have my books and my poetry to protect me."

Were love rational, I might have been persuaded by any number of these suitors and the ones who followed in college – those talented, intelligent, charming people who I've been friends with through the years, shared intimate moments with, watched B-movies with on rainy Saturday afternoons, ate Waldorf salads with and then did the dishes with in a quiet kitchen where the only sound was the swish of sudsy water. *People* who thought they loved me or who would have at least liked the opportunity to try loving me and whom I ultimately disappointed or grew weary of.

It is difficult feeling obliged to love someone. It is especially difficult when you do love that person, *just not that way.*

> *The most amusing or instructive companion is at best like a favourite volume, that we wish after a time to lay upon the shelf; but as our friends are not always willing to be laid there, this produces a misunderstanding and ill-blood between us.*

> —William Hazlitt

I TOLD MYSELF THROUGH all those years that my refusals, my willingness to remain detached and disinterested was a form of love, as it was the mildest possible disappointment, to make sure they knew there was no chance. I see now what I was not mature enough to know then: I was only shielding myself.

LOST, DEPLETED, USED UP, drained, exhausted, gone, given up, wasted, forgotten, forfeited, failed, fallen, fell short,

divested, misplaced, passed up, missing, off-track, dis-
oriented, irrevocable, lacking, strayed, vanished, absent,
absorbed, adrift, astray, bewildered, overcome, perplexed,
spellbound, misled, unredeemed, wayward, without, took
a beating, took a loss, took the heat, kissed goodbye, came
up short, wiped out, went out of business, bombed it, fell
between the cracks, away at sea, down the drain, fell on
deaf ears, blew it.

I'VE LOST MORE THAN JUST the first draft of this essay.
There have been losses from the second first draft as well,
thanks to the revisionist's knife. In that second attempt,
I invoked the Bible: parables of lost sheep, coins, sons; a
God of Nothing Lost; be ye therefore perfect. But these
thoughts didn't flow evenly with the rest of my thoughts.
The messages of the apostles seemed too full for the small
net of my imperfect experience.

In a sense, all memories have been forgotten.

—Duff, via Shields

THERE IS NO WAY FOR YOU to get the whole truth of these
essays. I pull these thoughts and experiences from my own
mind, from the fragmented pieces of my own memory,
where the lines are blurry and dull, the colors muted, even
if I try to recall them vividly. You only have the details
I've included, which will mix with your own memories or
imaginings of the place, and then you will have your own
version of the story. Your image of my mother standing
on the banks of the river will look one way, and my image
another, and we'll both be right for our own sakes, but
neither of us will grasp the full truth, which can only ever
be experienced in the moment. Even as I remember it, I

have lost details, remembering my mother older than she was at the time, her hair color slightly off.

Perhaps you might imagine the coldness of the sun-drenched water that swept my shoes away, or empathize with the delightful frustration that spread through my body when I lost this essay's beginnings, but I find it hard to believe you'll taste the bitterness of the words in my mouth when I told my friend that I didn't love her. I hardly tasted it myself.

MONTAIGNE HAS SAID THAT HE did not make his book so much as his book made him, and now that I am writing this essay – revising this essay – I find myself coming closer and closer to myself. To me, this is the real miracle of the essay, the microscope, the self-scrutiny. With each new draft, I lose my inhibitions and become more willing to see what I wouldn't look at before, prepared to lose my pride and examine in the light the parts I kept hidden from those who least deserved the shade.

MOST FRUSTRATING OF ALL, are the parts of the first draft that I've entirely forgotten. I have no idea what I have completely lost. I am sure it was brilliant, even transcendent. Probably the best thing I've ever written. But when I try to recall it now, there is only a quiet place in my mind, a cemetery of thought where even the gravestones have worn away and are indistinguishable from river stones, the grass has died to a yellow shag carpet, and the gate rusted down to nothing.

ALMOST TWO YEARS BEFORE that conversation in the street, there was a party at my house. She stayed after to help clean up. I knew why she was lingering. I dreaded a private conversation with her, but I took comfort in knowing that my roommates were close at hand. But eventually the cups were in the cupboards, the dishes in the dishwasher, and the roommates in their rooms, and she was still around. She asked if we could talk.

I sat in the corner of the large L-sofa; she sat on the coffee table, directly in front of me, cornering me. I knew what was coming because I had known she was interested in me for a while.

"I like you," she said, then surprised me by bolting to the door, fumbling with the bolt. She half tripped as she stumbled into the darkness, then turned, her hand still on the knob, her feet on the steps below.

"Like, really, *really* like you."

She closed the door and was gone before I'd processed the scene, her words lingering like a glass slipper on the steps, an invitation to pursue.

But how did Charming react? He set his precedent for silence and said nothing. He let the whole thing stew, and she didn't bring it up again for two years. And what did he do with the glass slipper? He laid it on the shelf where he kept the dusty others, where he can muse on them while he thinks about the women he's hurt, while essaying to account for his own losses, never considering until it is too late what others have given up.

IF I COULD RECALL WHAT I'd written in that first draft, this is where I might have mentioned the Beatles' lyrics about love gone cold and people who gain the world but lose their soul.

She is still a dear friend, and I could tell you more about her, about our relationship past and present, about the close relationship she had with my brother after I turned her down, about so many nights out for sushi. I could even tell you more about lost shoes, lost keys, and lost love, but these essays can't contain everything, even though, like Montaigne, I'm driven to continually revise and add. But even with the new material, the story will never be true, though it was true once, by which I mean that the events actually happened, and the regret for my callousness was real. But I've lost the edge on the regret, the main impetus for including her story, and where I once felt guilty for her unrequited love, now I feel guilty for re-exposing her pain and my lack of interest. We've both lost the people we were then, lost them to time, to new relationships, to a kind of forgiveness. So, no, I don't excuse myself; I see now that my childishness gained me nothing except the experience of it, but also that, like a child's shoe in a vast river, some ripples are quickly smoothed.

OF COMPLICATED THEMES

An essay elucidating notions I've had, the ideas of others, and interesting facts about squirrels.

(after David Shields' *Reality Hunger*)

1.
I dislike the request "Tell me a story." Almost every girl I've dated has asked me this. I don't know if this is indicative of all relationships, if it is just something people like asking the writers in their life, or if I've just dated girls who like a good story, but I do not like the request. When they ask me for the story I freeze up, go blank; things get awkward quickly. I am not a storyteller.

2.
Art is not a patent office; it is a conversation.

3.
When a squirrel is being pursued, she will zig-zag back and forth in an attempt to confuse the predator. If she is in a tree, she will circle around it, changing directions several times, always on the opposite side of the trunk from the animal persuing her. These evasive maneuvers work well with cats and better with dogs.

4.
Stability isn't always much to be desired.

5.

We live surrounded by ideas and objects infinitely more ancient than we imagine; and yet at the same time everything is in motion.

6.

Consider the circumvolutions of the human mind, where no short or direct route exists.

7.

The more you look at anything, the more tangled it becomes. We explore in order to bind.

8.

At a lecture I attended, Brian Doyle looked me in the eyes, put his hand on my shoulder, and in his nasally voice said, "Whatever you're sure of, don't be."

9.

The simplest answer is usually the correct one.

10.

Squirrels will sample every tree in their range. While it would make sense that they would just stick to the tree with the best or most abundant nuts, squirrels are not content to merely choose after one tasting. They will roam throughout their territory, trying every tree, eating more if they like what they find, but then they will move on again, never certain that they have the best. They return to each tree throughout the season; as the tree's nuts develop and change, each sampling brings a new taste and a new judgment.

11.

Please forgive me if I take an indirect route to answers, or perhaps, to more questions.

12.

We should make some concessions to the simple authority of the common laws of Nature but not allow ourselves to be swept tyrannously away by her: Reason alone must govern our inclinations.

13.

Opposition is true friendship.

14.

When the conversation is lively enough, I can talk endlessly, spouting story after story. If you tell a story about your dog, I will tell you how I once trained a dog to army crawl, or how my parents' dog loves to chase Frank, the squirrel that lives near my grandparents' cabin in the Uinta mountains, or maybe I'll shift to cats and talk about how one of my cats will play fetch like a dog. If you get me going, there isn't a story I can't one-up.

15.

In stories, you tell what you know. In essays, you explore what you want to know.

16.

When I was young, I could remember anything, whether it had happened or not. Now that I am getting older, I can only remember the latter.

17.

A squirrel's selection of food is neither simple nor random. The squirrel considers her options: acorns, pinecones, walnuts, mushrooms, etc. She will find the food that provides the most energy for the least amount of energy spent, all while calculating the likely presence of predators. A squirrel's life is summed up in an algorithm of innumerable variables. She is opportunistic but calculating. The number one cause of death for squirrels: starvation.

18.

A bad essay tells stories about people instead of elucidating the matter at hand.

19.

A girl in high school told me that she (and the rest of our friends, too, she assured me) hated talking with me because every time anyone said anything I would contradict them. She went so far as to give proof: "All of your sentences start with 'Actually...' or 'Yes, but...'"

20.

My object was to learn, not to preach.

21.

I do not understand. I pause. I examine.
That first sentence is not a complaint or even a condition. It is a declaration.

22.

When a squirrel has found food, she examines it carefully. First, she examines the smell, making sure that the nut is still good, that the food hasn't rotted. Then, she carefully scrapes her teeth over every crevice of the nut's shell. If the nut is cracked, the squirrel will eat it. If the shell is still whole, the squirrel will bury it for later use.

23.
When all has been said, you never talk about yourself without loss: condemn yourself and you are always believed: praise yourself and you never are.

24.
We are nothing if we don't have stories.

25.
We are double within ourselves. We do not believe what we believe. We are capable of being in uncertainties without reaching after fact and reason.

26.
An essay is always about something else.

27.
I told a (recently ex-)girlfriend how uncomfortable on-the-spot storytelling made me, but I stumbled over what to call my conversation style, poorly paraphrasing William Hazlitt's assertion that good writers don't make good orators. "I don't tell stories," I said, "I complicate themes."

28.
Contradictory judgments neither offend me nor irritate me: they merely wake me up and provide me with exercise. We avoid being corrected: we ought to come forward and

accept it, especially when it comes from conversation not a lecture.

29.
Make everything as simple as possible, but not simpler.

30.
I'm hard-pressed to tell stories about myself, but it is easy to make-up stories about others. We're trained from birth to look and judge, to imply, and the stories we tell about others are the mirrors we use to examine ourselves.

31.
A YouTube video shows a squirrel navigating a Rube Goldberg machine. It is an intricately involved obstacle course: a tightrope, several long jumps to otherwise-inaccessible platforms, a slide, a windmill, narrow tubes, at the end of which are some peanuts.

32.
Examine all things intensely and relentlessly. Probe and search each object. Do not leave it, do not course over it, as if it were understood, but instead follow it down until you see it in the mystery of its own specificity.

33.
Yes, but I just like looking at things from a different point of view. I am not committed to my contradictions.

34.
I recently posted on Facebook how much I hated it when girlfriends asked me to tell them a story. One ex responded

by telling me a story about the squirrel she chased in the metro, and how it ran back and forth through the station. My most recent ex responded by posting on her blog about how much she enjoyed reading fiction and not having to hear anything about essays or squirrels now that she was single, and my only other ex responded in jest by asking me to tell her a story. So, I told her:

This one time I was driving on a forest road and a squirrel zig-zagged under my car. I wanted to swerve, but that would have meant death to the car, so instead I hit the squirrel. The surprising part was that I felt no guilt.

35.
There is nothing in life so simple that a human mind can't make it more complex.

36.
When a squirrel buries nuts, she does so with a knowing distrust. She will bury one nut, then another, then return to the first to make sure that it is still there, but, having doubted the safety of the hiding spot, she will rebury her treasure somewhere else. The squirrel will bury each nut three or four times before she is content. And even then, once the horde is cached away, the squirrel rechecks each nut, repositioning as needed.

37.
The essay functions the way a metaphor functions, by negotiating the space between two items.

38.
Honesty is often artless. Lying is the highest form of art.

39.
Actually, all art is quite useless.

40.
It seemed to me that the greatest favor I could do for my mind was to leave it in total idleness, caring for itself, concerned only with itself, calmly thinking of itself. But I find that on the contrary it bolted off like a runaway horse, taking far more trouble over itself than it ever did anyone else; it gives birth to so many chimeras and fantastic monstrosities, one after the other, without order or fitness, that, so as to contemplate at ease their oddness and their strangeness, I begin to make a record of them, hoping in time to make my mind ashamed of itself.

41.
You cannot reason with an unreasonable being.

42.
The only art is the one that questions itself.

43.
The surprising number of car incidents resulting in squirrel fatalities is simply explained: the crisscrossing does nothing to dissuade a car.

44.
My new girlfriend, Kirsten, saw the Facebook post about hating storytelling just before our first date, and she has never asked me to tell her a story. Instead, she asks, "What are you thinking about?" or "Will you read me an essay?" We are getting along just fine.

TRAINS IN THE NIGHT

My new house is close to the railroad tracks that cut through the city's lower south side. When insomnia keeps me awake, I hear the trains' hooting calls, each one a warning to cars and late-night ramblers that they are passing by, crossing through, and I cannot sleep until their wailing whistles subside.

I AWOKE ONE NIGHT IN A TERROR; the house's shadows trembling as a train passed by and an engineer with no mercy yanked the whistle cord, producing one long scream in the night. I imagined the engineer in his engine, his grimace at the dark that surrounded him, glaring at the streetlights that winked at his slow-moving train. Everyone within blocks of the tracks jolted awake, but he didn't care. I heard this particular engineer several times: the angry call of his whistle gave him away. Some nights, when his whistle was particularly loud and I was bitter about lost sleep, I imagined that his wife had just left him, and I created for him a home as dark and cold as the night through which he passed. His whistle screamed to the neighborhood, and the people were forced to listen. But other nights, the nights when I am already awake and alone in the dark of my room, I imagine that the whistle is anxious, not angry: the engineer's wife waits for him at home; she's just returned from her night job as a police dispatcher. She makes three sunny-side-up eggs, two for him and one for her, and butters three pieces of toast, one for him and two for her, and pours two tall glasses of cold orange juice. After breakfast, they retire to bed and, curled together, sleep through the sunlit hours.

BUT DURING THE DAY, the trains sound distant. Even at the bus stop, much closer to the tracks, I only faintly hear them over the sounds of traffic and birdsong. And the bus, too, has its own hissing, rumbling noise, which masks the sounds of even the closest trains. The people on the bus and I have grown accustomed to this noise, and to each other, having seen each other so often that we've become caricatures to each other: the old unshaven man whose fingers constantly fidget, whose pot belly extends below his shirt; the tiny woman wearing a *Mi Rancherito* Mexican Restaurant polo, who pays her fare in nickels and dimes; the twenty-something guy with arms sleeved in muddled tattoos, who wears a University of Utah hoodie on cold mornings; the thin young woman with a sparkling wedding band, whose long, straight hair hides her face; the middle-aged woman whose body flows over the seat of her motorized wheelchair; a young fidgety man who stares a little too long at each passenger as they board; and me, the grad student with a second-hand sports coat and a squirrel patch on my bookbag. These people all live close to the tracks, too, and I wonder how they sleep. But nobody talks about the trains. No one talks at all. We try to keep our eyes watching the window or beyond, feeling claustrophobic in our proximities as the sun crests the mountains.

ANOTHER ENGINE DRIVER is matter-of-fact in her pulling of the cord: three short cacophonous bursts, each the same length, a rhythm I could appreciate as I lay not sleeping, looking up at the ceiling. She pulls hard and releases quickly; her arm pumping three times in rapid succession. She knows that people are sleeping, that the woman with the sparkling wedding ring and her husband are together in bed after their baby is *finally* asleep, praying the rumbling pitch won't stir her; that the tattooed man is just barely passing out after a night of hard studying; that the restaurant worker must rise in less than an hour to make breakfast for her family before leaving for *Mi Rancherito* where she will make meals for smiling strangers; that I did not sleep but fitfully all night and was just barely sliding into sleep. She knows all this, knows we in our houses have our sleepless concerns, but she has hers, too. She gives no defense for the way things are. She knows that her charge pushes through the middle of our quiet night, but still, the whistle must be whistled.

ONE OVERCAST AFTERNOON I walked down to the tracks perchance to see a train, which I didn't. The neighborhood appeared to be empty; I passed numerous overgrown lawns and weedy gardens. The highway humming in the distance and the birds singing in tangled trees provided the only accompaniment to my feet's thumping cadence. I stepped onto the concrete train platform with a plexiglass gazebo etched in years of teenage delinquency. An itinerary taped to the glass told me that the passenger trains that rolled through twice each night went from Chicago to San Francisco. Another poster showed two teenagers fishing off a railroad bridge, coolers of beer at their feet, unaware of the large train looming behind them. I turned away from the poster and toward my house. Two older ladies, a mother and grandmother, had come out to sit on the crumbling steps of the peeling house that faced the tracks. Several children played with a rotting pool table under a large oak tree, and I smiled at them from my place on the sidewalk. The women nodded from behind their fence but kept speaking only to each other.

I'M STILL THINKING OF THAT POSTER, and tonight, another engineer: His whistle builds in a slow crescendo and dies away with a mournful coda; I only hear the sound because I am already awake and waiting for the morning. He starts with his fingers lightly on the cable, just a touch before he adds more pressure, then, slowly, more, and as the sound peaks he's already letting go, just as slowly. His is the train in the poster, and he knows the importance of the whistle. Without the warning, cars will run across the tracks too late, or teenagers, high or drunk or stupid, won't get off the tracks. He has felt the train shudder with a sickening thud as those teenagers with the fish and the beer died on his watch. It wasn't his fault. He knows it's not his fault; the police, his partner, the company lawyers and grief counselors, his pastor, and the teens' families have all told him that it wasn't his fault. There was nothing he could do. The track had already been laid, the velocity of the train beyond his control. He has made his peace with the families and God and himself, but when he is alone with his thoughts on the train in the night the whistle builds and falls with his remorse. He whistles a warning and an apology both, a whistling wave that breaks on us all, and all we can do is listen.

TRIPTYCH: A STUDY IN COMFORT

1.

Nearly every evening, the same tableau: We recline in the second-hand sofas of my living room; we each occupy separate couches with clouds of papers spread across the cushions. Your fingers, pressed to your laptop, type in a student's grade. My own, so far from your body, hold a pen, scribble notes for tomorrow's lecture. Our heads bend at parallel angles, eyes down in concentration. Our bare feet support themselves on the IKEA coffee table, almost touching. Occasionally, our toes do touch, mostly accidentally, but sometimes on purpose as my mind wanders your body and our eyes lift, our worlds interrupted with flirtatious smiles.

2.

We are headed to your brother's house for Sunday dinner, something we do now that we are a couple, driving south on I-15, listening to Mumford and Son's first album, the only CD we listened to the first three months we dated. You look over your shoulder, shift lanes, and tell me about your counseling classes, your left hand on the wheel, the right alternating between motioning in the air, touching your heart, and tucking your hair behind your ear. Your class had interviewed marginalized people, and discussing the trans and gay people you'd spoken with led to your trouble with the cultural limitations of gender and the conservative bent of our childhoods; your head turns to me, eyes on me, then back on the road. My arms are at my side, seemingly at a restful angle on the arm rest, but they are rigid. My eyes are on you, intent, afraid to look away, lest you see in me what I've concealed.

You wonder to me about our church's assertion that "gender is eternal." Not that you doubt an eternal something about ourselves, but are troubled by *eternal*'s apparent meaning: fixed, binary, heteronormative. Of course, we didn't have this specific language back then. We were young, virgin, not yet accustomed to critical discourse but headed in that direction, side by side in your Honda CR-V. All we know in this scene is that the *eternal* pronouncement itched. You told me about an older gay man, also raised Mormon, who had said he "could have gone either way," if only he'd had some empathy, and I notice that you are expressing, giving, that sort of empathy now, at seventy-five miles per hour, due south. You continue to talk, and I listen, hardly saying anything, though I see in your thoughts the formation of my own, words I'd never expressed lest I free myself from the bounds of the binary. As we exit the freeway, you are bold—this early in our relationship, and living in the heart of Mormon conservatism, you couldn't have known well my politics—you proclaim your conviction that gender and sexuality are spectrums. I nod in agreement, casually, as if to suggest the ideas are indeed intellectually interesting and that I agree, not as though my world is tilting. No one has ever spoken to me about this before, and in return, I have not spoken to them. At the exact moment we turn left from the off-ramp and proceeded under the overpass, I understand that were I to show myself, you would see me, and that I can trust you, which is also when I see that I might love you. You will understand as I do that longing is body and love is soul, a lesson I've hidden away but relearn as you accelerate and say aloud what I will never utter for fear of what I might lose or let loose.

3.

Once we finish grading, we collect our various papers into their respective piles and bring our whole bodies together on just one couch. Your body pressed against mine, your legs curl up on the cushions. Your breasts press to my side as my lips and tongue read from one of the many books I've been assigned. My free arm wraps around you, where it can rest on your back or hip, and your head leans on my shoulder; your left hand snakes just under the open collar of my shirt and your fingers play with the hair of my chest. My whole body tingles with that chaste touch, craves it, sinks into its suggestiveness, a suggestion of intimacy.

POINTS OF TANGENCY

A tangent: any line that touches a circle or curved line at only one point; that point is called the *point of tangency*. For one moment—a moment infinitely brief, measurable only in mathematics and imaginations—the two distinct and separate lines are in the same space, moving in the same direction at the same velocity.

LAST WEEK, I RECEIVED two books as gifts. The first book, a belated Christmas present from my father and step-mother, was Anne Fadiman's *Ex Libris: Confessions of a Common Reader*.

My step-mom purchased the book on Amazon from a third-party seller who said the book was "GREAT!.***BRAND NEW***... CLEAN,CRISP,TIGHT...WITH DUST COVER. VERY NICE BOOK". The invoice was personalized with a note that said "Thanks, Best Regardly." in large, loopy handwriting.

I'd enjoyed Fadiman's other work, so I was excited to have this one, especially a copy that was ***BRAND NEW*** and CLEAN,CRISP,TIGHT, though I don't really know what the seller meant by calling a book "TIGHT." And I was surprised to find it wasn't exactly brand new, either. The inside corner of the dust jacket was snipped where the price had been, leaving only the

"Cana" of *Canada* intact. And, what's more, the name "Andy Rogers" was neatly written in green crayon—well, as neatly as crayon allows—on the ex libris provided in the inside cover. I knew my stepmom would have been upset to learn the book was not exactly as ***BRAND NEW*** as advertised, so I didn't mention this when I called to thank her.

I was not disappointed. I love used books; I'm fascinated by the idea that someone else had held this book and leafed through it. I can't stop wondering, *Who is this Andy Rogers?*

There is no way to know for certain, but Google has several suggestions: He is a "worship Leader and singer songwriter" from Ireland's Causeway Coast who enjoys "adventures in missional, 'Guerilla' Worship" and a photojournalist from Seattle who took a series of pictures about underground music concerts in DC. He's also a wedding photographer from Melbourne, Australia, a member of the Tampa Bay Lightning, and a Scottish footballer. And he is a ceramic artist in Maryville, Missouri, who says that "the most import thing an artist can do is be true to, and explore themselves," and whose "stimulation is, and always has been, found in the untouched areas around us."

Facebook suggests Andy Rogers is a young man from Texas, but it only brought up this profile first because that Andy Rogers knows my friend Steve's wife, Maria. There are other Facebook options, too: Andy Rogers is often a white teen striking a dramatic pose in a bedroom, sometimes a fat man with a goatee, sometimes a thirty-something black man with dreads whose favorite quotation is "GOD FIRST," who posted "NEW START" on Jan 15, to which someone named Lyn Adams replied "thank god."

He's also a white family man—several of him have pictures with small, happy children. He lives in Louisville and likes '80s hair bands, and he lives in Easthampton and likes massages. Sometimes he's gay, but mostly he's straight. He's usually young and handsome, though not always.

Of the 304 Andy Rogerses on Facebook at the time of writing, not one of them mentioned Anne Fadiman or green crayons in the limited profiles I could see. There are no other markings in the book, no other clues, except for Anne Fadiman's words themselves, which maybe Andy Rogers found as entertaining as I did, which I suppose was the point of this whole tangent—that when I read the book, I am in the same space that Andy Rogers once was or might have been. I don't even know if he got past the cover where he inscribed his name; for all I know someone else inscribed his name for him.

And though I am a white, straight-acting closeted bisexual, nonathletic, superficial Christian, handsome-ish, writer, photographer, and California native in a relationship with a woman, Andy Rogers is only those things some of the time and not all at the same time; but when I read *Ex Libris*—which I did with my girlfriend, she stretched out across my couch with her head resting on my lap as I read aloud—I am a reader as he was once a reader. And now that he has discarded the book, he will become part of the "long chain of readers" that Fadiman herself talks about, reveling in the knowledge that someone else has graced the pages of the used books she essays upon.

I SUPPOSE PEOPLE MIGHT think it's creepy to look through strangers' Facebook profiles and glimpse the tidbits they have given the world, but I enjoy it. Many people do. In fact, when my girlfriend confessed to Facebook stalking me before we actually got to know each other, I didn't think it weird. I am a shameless Facebook stalker. I love it when I find someone like Andy Rogers in Texas who has a friend in common with me here in Utah. I enjoy it even more when I can find enough snippets of someone's life to make up stories, to put small pieces together for drama that doesn't exist, for, in the words of Ann Beattie, "any life will seem dramatic if you omit mention of most of it." And what are social networks if not a sequence of careful omissions?

Once, when Facebook was young and still a year or two from taking off, I was exploring the world via Google Maps, and I came across Sublette, Kansas. I did a quick search for Sublette on Google and found that it had a population of 1,592 as of the 2000 census, and that it was named for William Lewis Sublette, a French-Huguenot fur trapper the indigenous people called "Cut Face," which sounds like the title for a cheap horror film or maybe a Dick Tracy villain.

After I found Sublette, it was only a matter of time before I discovered Pumpkin Paradise, LLC, the only tourist attraction in town. Pumpkin Paradise features corn mazes, wagon rides, and a pumpkin catapult. The owner is Steve Weidner. I looked up Steve and found that he was also on the Emergency Medical Response committee and a member of the graveyard council, which seemed like a conflict of interest.

By looking for more about Steve, I found his name on a court case. I learned the graveyard was sued by a couple who wanted to build a monument for unborn babies, a way to comfort parents who had lost children to "miscarriage, stillbirth and abortion," but the bylaws stated that only graves representing actual bodies could be placed in the cemetery, and the court ruled in favor of the bylaws, removing the monument, which quoted Isaiah:

I WILL NEVER FORGET YOU. SEE, UPON THE PALMS OF MY HANDS I HAVE WRITTEN YOUR NAME

I didn't like Steve as much after that, even though there was nothing in the court documents that suggested he was particularly adamant about the ruling. Still, it wasn't long before the details about the graveyard and the pumpkins led to Steve becoming the main character of a Halloween fantasy in my head, a story in which he hires zombies from the graveyard to work the pumpkin farm, but then his daughter falls in love with one of the zombies, which Steve naturally disapproves of, because he doesn't want his family to know that he's been using his placement on the Emergency Response team to kill off young, able-bodied men for cheap labor.

A FEW WEEKS AGO, I bought a used coat, a heavy winter coat with lots of pockets, from a Lost and Found sale. Inside one of the pockets I discovered an airline ticket that had been torn in half. The ticket was for one Sevak Tsaturyan, who was flying from Salt Lake City to St. Louis on Tuesday, November 4, 2008.

I knew all of the items I had just purchased—an umbrella, a beanie, two coats—had been lost. And I knew the Lost and Found department only sells things that have been unclaimed for quite a few months. But here I knew the name of the person who used to own this coat, so I felt a sort of guilt, as though I were stealing, even though I learned in an introductory law class that anything bought in good faith belongs to the buyer, even if the seller acquired the item in dubious circumstances. So, my guilt had nothing to do with the legality of my purchase, but more to do with my immediate connection to these random people whose names appear in the periphery of my life, names I seem to pull out of my pocket as though it were some sort of magic trick meant to amaze only me.

Naturally, I looked Sevak up, finding him on Facebook. We have four friends in common. We both attended graduate school at Brigham Young University in Utah, Sevak in the MBA program and me in the MFA. It looks like he had already graduated when I bought the coat; he now lives in California. He looks well enough off from his pictures and doesn't appear to be freezing.

I just sent him a Facebook message to let him know I have the coat and to ask why he flew to St. Louis all those years ago. I'll wait for his response. This may be a good time to get a drink, or use the restroom…

…OKAY, SEVAK HAS REPLIED. He said I can keep the coat (so generous!), but now that he knows his name was in the pocket, he wishes the Lost and Found people had checked more thoroughly.

The truth is, he doesn't remember losing the coat; all he remembers is that he had to buy a new one. He flew to St. Louis for a job interview, and the flight was on the day of the elections. He told me he didn't do well in the interview because he was upset about Obama's win. He asked me what the coat looks like, and in my reply I gave him a description and told him I didn't think the Lost and Found people really checked the inner pockets, citing the fact that the other coat I'd purchased that day, a blazer, had almost of year's worth of tithing receipts in its inner breast pocket for one Timothy Bishop. I didn't tell Sevak that I didn't contact Timothy because knowing his tithing statements seemed too personal and sacred an invasion, nor that I had voted for Obama. We share a coat but not the same political outlook.

EVEN BEFORE ANDY AND SEVAK AND TIMOTHY, I had already been pondering the random items in my possession that had someone else's name on them. I had recently gone to the library to do some research, and I found a book titled *North American Tree Squirrels*. On the inside cover was the following bookplate:

BRIGHAM YOUNG UNIVERSITY
is pleased to place this volume in the
HAROLD B. LEE LIBRARY
in memory of
Melvin H. Leavitt
A VALUED ALUMNUS OF BYU

I couldn't rest until I figured out who Melvin was and why he got to have his name in a book about squirrels.

I looked him up on the BYU website, but found no mention of him, making me wonder if he could really be that "valued." An Internet search found his BYU yearbook picture from 1927, but it would have cost me $25/

year to join some site, which I was pretty sure would have spammed my email account for the next infinity, so I didn't join. Who was this Melvin, and how did a book about squirrels come to be donated in his honor?

The how part was simple: I asked a librarian how someone gets a book donated in their name—let's be honest, I was jealous of Melvin and wanted to see how I could get a squirrel book donated for me—and they said that sometimes when people die or have a significant birthday, they ask people to donate money to the library, and then the library uses the money however they see fit. Which meant that Melvin probably didn't have anything to do with squirrels, he was just lucky.

Eventually, thanks to Google, I did track him down, or at least a free picture of him with a bit of biography from a genealogy book that was written in the '60s. He was born and raised in Bunkerville, Nevada, and went to BYU to study agriculture. From there he moved back and forth between Reno, Nevada, and Northern Idaho, and was a bishop of his local LDS congregations in both places.

I'm not sure what happened to him since. The biography ends with him alive and well in Reno. My Internet search says there is a 107-year-old man named Melvin Leavitt living in Nampa, Idaho, but they want to charge me $10.95 per month to access an "unlimited profile," which will probably tell me little more than his name and how old he is, but maybe not even that, because the local phone books don't say anything about a Melvin Leavitt in Nampa or Reno.

Interestingly, there is a Melvin Leavitt currently residing in Reno, Idaho, but he was far too young to be the one I was looking for. The most I have of the one I sought is that brief bio and a picture of him with his family: three sons, two daughters, and his wife. None of them are particularly interesting people to look at, but his name crossed my path and I can't leave him alone.

Which is silly, I guess, because I could call the number I got from the phone book and ask if this is the Melvin Leavitt who used to live in Nevada, who is more than 100 years old. And when he says that it is in fact him, why am I calling, I would say I saw his name on the inside of a book about squirrels, and, well, I just really like squirrels. And another random person I looked up once had written that the most import thing an artist can do is to explore themselves, and that stimulation is found in the untouched areas around us, which for me means that I explore those areas around me that would otherwise go unnoticed.

WHEN WE SPEAK OF TANGENTS in casual conversation, when we use *tangent* in a non-mathematical sense, we generally mean "departure." We go off on tangents, we speak tangentially, we essay through artistic tangents. Modern usage and dictionaries have accepted this new definition, but this use itself is a departure from the original meaning.

Tangent comes from the Latin *tangere*: "to touch." It is not "departing from" but "coming to." We see similarities in *tangent*'s close cousins *tangible, tact,* and *tactile.* Less obvious are *attain,* to reach after and touch; *contagion,* literally "with touching"; and *contingent* with its archaic sibling *pertingent.* In the negative, we get *integer,* whole or untouched, and from there we also get *entire* and *intact.*

Tangere has entered art and medicine through an uncommon tangency, through the phrase *noli me tangere,* which means, "Don't touch me." In medicine this refers to contagious skin diseases in which the patient should remain entirely untouched. In a similar vein, *noli me tangere* also refers to artistic representations of Christ outside the garden tomb. In this scene, Mary Magdalene would throw her arms around her resurrected Lord or kiss his feet to worship him, but he forbids her to touch him, saying he has not yet ascended to Heaven, and then, having shown himself alive though denying her tangential urges, he departs.

I KNEW A MAN AT CHURCH who looked up people's information as a hobby. Brother Goodwin was a professional genealogist who specialized in inheritance claims, so he had access to those email-spamming websites that gave people's background facts. He would use them to look up information for his clients, but also for the random people he met.

I was a missionary at the time, and I would go door to door asking people if they wanted to learn about our church. One day a family in Brother Goodwin's neighborhood seemed particularly interested; later that night I mentioned the family to Brother Goodwin when I called him about other church matters. He asked who the family was, so I told him their name.

"Oh, they live on Ash Street, and before that lived in Texas?"

"Yeah, that's them. You know them?"

"No, I just looked them up. Do you want to know how much they pay in taxes?"

I didn't. Well, I did, but thought maybe it would be unprofessional while I was trying to teach about the church. "Render unto Caesar...," etc.

It was that way with everyone for Brother Goodwin. Our responsibilities at church often overlapped, and whenever we visited people together, he always seemed to know details about their lives, both because he asked them directly and because he looked them up. Perhaps he was just nosy like me, but I suspected his fascination came from an actual concern for other people, a real compassion for strangers and friends alike and genuine interest in their lives. I, on that other hand, am content to garner what I can and make up the rest. The gleaning is for my own benefit. The harvest solipsistic.

I attended a funeral with Brother Goodwin once, for a man in our congregation who had been hospitalized for several years, and whom we each visited weekly. The man's relatives were Jehovah's Witnesses, but they were nice enough to invite some of his Mormon friends to the wake, and as we chatted with strangers and ate from the buffet laid out in a humble home, someone asked Brother Goodwin if he had any children, and he said that he didn't.

"Why not?" the woman asked.

"Well, we tried, and we tried, but it just never happened."

And in that moment, I felt embarrassed for Brother Goodwin—I admit that I thought of him and his wife trying and trying, and I blushed. But I was also sad for him, this man who connected himself to everything and everyone, who was the first to volunteer to help a stranger but who also looked up their names in his databases and found out their intimate details, not because he was a snoop, but because he liked people. And yet, despite trying and trying, he passed this love on only through those he touched.

Several years later, Brother Goodwin died of a heart attack, though it's hard to imagine him with a failing of the heart. He went quickly, from what a friend told me, literally dropped dead.

A FEW DAYS AGO, I WAS in the optometrist's office waiting for my appointment. I didn't find a magazine I wanted to look at, so I was absent-mindedly contemplating Melvin Leavitt and the ticket stub from my coat, when I became aware of the web of connections there in the office. Someone had made the mirror; someone had installed the lights; the counters and cabinets were made by someone else; and then I saw the hundreds of frames hanging in the cabinets, and I knew that someone had put each frame on display, and someone else had designed them. The pair of Jones New York frames I ultimately chose must have been tried on by someone else, and the five other pairs I tried on but didn't buy will be tried on by five more people each, but only one person will take each of those pairs home, and with it the indelible traces of my invisible past. The receptionist's computer, the chair I was sitting on, the magazines on the end table, the clothes I was wearing...

Eventually, I had to stop because I got dizzy. There is no end to such thinking.

Which brings me to the second book I received last week. My friend and professor Pat Madden gave me a copy of Scott Russell Sanders's *The Paradise of Bombs*, which had been signed by the author:

> *For Gary Hatch—*
> *my first collection of essays,*
> *where I revealed my apprenticeship*
> *to this marvelous form—*
> *Scott R. Sanders*
> *16 Oct 2009*

Such signatures—from the author to some other person—are almost as exciting as having the author sign it for you, because it has all the implications of other used books, but also traces its pedigree back to the author himself. In *Ex Libris*, Fadiman also revels in such finds,

> *Such holy relics of literary tangency eclipse all other factors: binding, edition, rarity, condition. 'The meanest, most draggle-tailed, foxed, flead, dog's-eared drop of a volume' ... is instantly transfigured by an inscription with a sufficiently distinguished pedigree.*

The book I'd received was actually in pretty good condition, but its signature made it all the more exciting because I had recently heard the story of Gary Hatch, though I had never met him.

An English professor at BYU in his 40s, with a successful career as a teacher, Gary Hatch was well liked by his colleagues, who remembered him as a voracious reader.

One day he told the Dean that he'd had a premonition he wouldn't be teaching at BYU by the end of the year. He didn't know why this would be the case, but he suggested the dean start looking for a replacement. A few months later, he came home early from a party, telling his wife he didn't feel well, and then he collapsed. He died a few hours later. Months afterward, with his wife's permission, the other professors distributed Gary's books among themselves, and when I told Pat that I wanted to read *The Paradise of Bombs*, he told me he had an extra copy and gave me the one he'd acquired from Gary's collection.

Other than the inscription from the author, there are no markings in the book. The binding is clean, neat, tight. The book looks brand new. I have no proof Gary actually read the book, only that he owned it once. To me, Sanders's inscription sounds perfunctory, and there is no sign of any real connection between the two men, but Pat told me that though Gary Hatch helped fund Scott Russell

Sanders's visit to campus, he'd missed the reading because of a scheduling conflict, and that when he went to greet the author, Mr. Sanders had already inscribed the passage for him, having prepared the book as a thank you. I imagine Mr. Sanders with the book some moments before, the pen hovering over the not-yet signed book, considering just what words to say.

And now the book rests beside me, a tangible prayer for Professor Hatch who has departed his short life, and who is only a part of mine because of that departing. Under contemplation, I see a universe of lines stretching forth from that book, an infinite web of paths curving, touching briefly and intangibly, moving in the same direction at the same speed for a time incalculable, before paths diverge in a fracturing web and the lines extend forever with infinite tangencies. And in the midst of all that, with his book in hand, I touch what I can never fully comprehend.

CLAY

The first time I entered the Museum of Peoples and Cultures, a few minutes early for a summer internship interview, I looked over the pottery collection from the long-departed city of Paquime, which, though now a maze of weather-eaten adobe walls and old, old dust in northern Mexico, was once a thriving cultural center. The inhabitants traded far to the extremes of their world, away from the heart of the desert to the sea, to the mountains and jungles. They worshiped Quetzalcoatl, the Plumed Serpent, to whom they beheaded macaws on a high sacrificial mound, a mound which, from above, looks like the severed head of the birds they idolized. They played a complex ball game, the rules now lost; the only remains of the game are the I-shaped ball court and the bones of the losing teams, who forfeited their lives to Quetzalcoatl. Once a thriving community, Paquime was simply abandoned; no violence or sudden drought adequately explains the exodus of its people. The homes, ball courts, sacrificial mounds, were already in ruins when the Spanish explored the area. *Casas Grandes*, the newcomers called the ghost city, Big Houses.

As I considered the pots before me, the ancient world seemed so impossibly distant. I thought of the hands that shaped the clay, painted it with red and black snakes, birds, toads, and geometric lines no human can now decipher.

Displayed with the larger pots were several tiny ones, the bowls of which were no bigger than a thumbprint. At first, I smirked at the small shaped clay. These minuscule pots were so insignificant beside the great city's other remnants, yet they displayed themselves as proudly as their elaborate companions.

I imagined how such mini-pots must have been made: No doubt a little girl's hands had once graced a lump of clay, her mother's discarded remnant, and squeezed it between her fingers, feeling the cool, moist clay mix into the warmth of her skin. She pressed her thumb into the ball and pinched the sides. Her mother, forming a pot shaped like a warrior clothed in jaguar skins, smiled at the attempt, remembering her own beginnings.

Before the mother took the pots to the kiln, she rounded out her daughter's little creations, making them symmetrical and even. With the clay in the fire, the little girl waited, waited, until finally—*finally*—the pots came out covered in ash and burnt a deep red, the color of macaw blood and desert mud. The mother showed the daughter how to polish the pottery: *Rub with these burnishing stones, smear it with this gritty slip, yes, yes, now scrape it, pull it back to smooth it, scrape, smooth, smooth.* During the evening meal the girl talked only of her vessels. Her father pulled the lump of baked clay to his eyes, admiring it, telling her that it was the finest pottery he had seen; he smiled at his little girl and then looked up to catch his wife's gleeful eyes and winked.

"These we will display for the world," he said, and placed them on a shelf near the door.

After the next cleaning, the girl stowed the pots in the woven basket that safeguarded her other treasures: a white snake skin from the dry wash, a copper bell her uncle brought from the south, a blue and red macaw feather, the tooth she lost the previous week.

The day her parents told her that they were leaving the city, the girl packed her treasures first.

"No, no," her mother said, "there is no room in the pack. There will be more snake skins where we are going. There will be more macaws. We will make more pots; there is always more clay."

And a few hundred years later, the Spaniards stood in awe, pausing in search for the Golden City to contemplate this dusty urban skeleton. What touched them most about the remnants and ruins? Did they sit in the walls' shade, sipping tepid water, looking over their shoulders for ghosts? Did they celebrate Mass among the earthen remains? And which of these pots did they also touch, adding to the ancient clay their own intangible legacy? Did they imagine a little girl weeping, as I did? Surely she wept more for the loss of these tiny treasures than for the city itself. She had merely inhabited the city—it has always been there—but she created this pot from nothing but clay. She must have felt the smooth clay between her fingers one last time, then one last time again, before reluctantly returning it to its place with the bell. Did she know? Surely, she knew that her little thumbprint pot would remain as cities crumbled, as the ages of men passed, as empires rose and fell.

THE COMMON AREA

It's 3:30 in the morning. I've been in Edinburgh for less than twenty-four hours, and I am still trying to recover from the jetlag, so I've come down to the hostel's common area to get a snack and do some writing. I didn't know when I came down that the hostel's kitchen was closed for the night, which means I can't get to my food, though I can see it through the tiny, scratched windows of the kitchen doors. I examined the vending machines, but they only take coins, and all I have are the crisp bills I picked up from the ATM at the airport. So, I sat down to write at the round tables. My notebook is sprawled out before me, a click pen in hand.

I've written just that far when I get up and try the kitchen doors a second time.

"The kitchen is closed." There is a man on the couch, and I am suddenly aware that either I had woken him, or he'd been silently watching me for some time.

I turn to look at him. He's wearing a faded t-shirt and shabby white briefs, his thin, flabby legs spread as though intentionally displaying his grimy underwear. He shifts around a bit, not uncomfortably, but perhaps uncertain how to act now that he's been caught. He sits on the couch a bit longer before hobbling out into the hall without saying anything more. I return to my notebook on the table.

Hunger isn't the only thing keeping me awake or driving me out of bed. I am tense and cold: the short blanket only barely covered my feet, and one of my roommates had opened the window. I could hear urban traffic all night. Sirens, people arguing drunkenly on the sidewalks, and raucous laughter all seemed menacing, as all such sounds do late at night in strange cities. The discomfort reminds me that I am here in Scotland for a "cultural experience," as a graduate student assistant for a study abroad program. But, despite my insecurities and insomnia, there is a charm to the sounds, too, and so I sit here essaying and trying to find meaning in these foreign sounds that are uncomfortable and inviting.

Now that I am writing, I can't even remember what my thoughts were before getting out of bed, but the straining for meaning in my contradictory reaction to the noise had something to do with it, a vague sense of a lightened darkness and a charming menace, just outside the window.

I recall, now, the many study abroad essays I've read as an editor of a student journal—so many cringy ones that I told my staff we wouldn't publish anything about study abroad programs—and I worry that I am just looking for the same shallow arguments I'd seen in those essays: Young American sees a new country for the first time, Young American feels like an outsider, Young American has an epiphany. Young American feels at home. Young American understands.

I don't feel like an outsider, but I've not explored much beyond the hostel, either, just wandered the streets for a few hours while I waited for the rest of my group to arrive. I had historical questions about the ruins on the hills, but nothing pressing. I admired the glassy exteriors of Edinburgh's skyscrapers, reveled in the green and rocky richness of the fortressed hills. But I can't help coming back to the fact that this is essentially my first time outside of the USA—except for the one day my dad and I crossed into Mexico to buy kitchen tiles when I was six, and an afternoon on the Canadian side of Niagara Falls just a few years ago—so in many ways I am Eager Young American, ready for Culture, the World, and Experience. I am trying to steer my thoughts away from the clichés conjured by my excitement and hopes, but I can't sleep because I am excited and hopeful. I want this to be the life-changing experience all writers hope for, where inspirations abound. Edinburgh seems ripe for such experiences, a city of complements and contradictions: the modern offices butt against ancient castles; new fashions against traditional foods; the mausoleum of David Hume next to a statue of Abraham Lincoln; a calm, friendly calico cat sitting on the steps of Calton Hill under a "Lost Cat" sign. This early in my trip, these details still entice me because I've grown neither callous nor comfortable.

While I've been noticing these contradictions, I've also been thinking about enthusiasm. On the flight from Chicago Midway to London Heathrow I sat next to Eliot, a first-rate Brit, not quite two years old. As the plane ferried out for takeoff, Eliot delightedly pointed out every airplane he saw, and since we were in an airport—the fifth busiest in the world—that was no small number.

"Airplane! Airplane!" His little pointer finger extended at the end of an outstretched arm as far as the seatbelt would allow him to go.

His mother apologized for his enthusiasm, but honestly, it was adorable, and as far as sitting next to a toddler on an airplane goes, not so bad.

A YOUNG MAN JUST WALKED into the common room carrying the smell of cigarettes with him. He stares at the vending machine and says, "No cigarettes?" He has a thick accent, one that I don't recognize, perhaps German. It's hard to tell from just two words. I shrug, but as I look up and consider the vending machines again, I recall my hunger. The young man turns away from me and studies the vending machine for a while but leaves without purchasing anything.

His cigarette musk lingers.

I'VE BEEN CONTEMPLATING ENTHUSIASM ever since sitting next to Eliot because I am concerned about my enthusiasm for squirrels. I behave around squirrels much as Eliot does around planes. ("Squirrel!" was my catchphrase long before Disney's Up was a thing). I've collected the paraphernalia to prove it: at least fifteen squirrel t-shirts, books on squirrel biology, lots of little squirrel ornaments, a tie, and a pair of boxers. My MFA thesis is squirrel themed. I sign my letters and some credit card receipts with a squirrel-shaped wiggle of a signature.

However, when I broke up with Kirsten, my girlfriend of eight months—or maybe ex-girlfriend now—just over a week ago, she asked me why I couldn't be as enthusiastic about her as I was for squirrels. It was not the main part of our disagreement, but it struck me hard nonetheless. Partially, it hurt because though squirrels were part of my identity, the thing everyone knew they could talk to me about—"I'm not obsessed," I would tell people, "I'm enthusiastic."—her jealousy of my enthusiasm for squirrels felt odd. I had thought she knew me better; I thought she could see through my superficial love for them. I thought that she, of all people, would have noticed that even with my enthusiasm, even in the pleasure I got from people talking to me about squirrels, even with all that, even I knew it was a silly fascination. An inside joke with the whole world. Were squirrels all to disappear, I would find something else to feed that eccentricity. I thought she understood that about me. Besides, who would want to be the object of such attention? Squirrels are completely unaware and unaffected by my devotion. They thrive and decline independent of my enthusiasm, so there's no harm done that I collect their pictures and horde t-shirts with their images. Who wants that in a boyfriend?

So, we're uncertain now, though it was good for so long. I apologized to her. We made up at Red Mango, her favorite frozen yogurt joint, where her order every time is pomegranate yogurt with mini chocolate chips and coconut mochi. We're a couple again, but that was only a few days ago, right before I left on this two-month trip to the British Isles, a trip I was only brave enough to take because Kirsten encouraged it, a trip for which I acquired my first passport, heading over the water, sitting next to Eliot, the plane enthusiast.

THE YOUNG GUY LOOKING for cigarettes has come back. He found some tobacco and came into the common area to roll his smokes. I don't have many friends who smoke. I've never seen anyone roll their own; seeing him do so now makes him seem like a connoisseur, so much more interesting than when he was just some guy looking for a cigarette from a vending machine. To be honest, I don't know if "rolling a smoke" is what one would actually say, nor do I know if rolling them makes one especially talented, but he seems adept. He introduces himself as Jimmy. He's French and is studying in Dundee.

"I'm drunk," Jimmy tells me, "and if I go to sleep, I will throw up. I heard that the Volunteer Arms is opening at seven." At first, I think the Volunteer Arms is a place for food, like a soup kitchen—*Arms* has me thinking *Salvation Army*, my early morning brain too slow to understand—but then he tells me that there will be a jukebox and that he just needs music. My next thought is a soup kitchen with a rocking dance scene before I realize he's talking about a club. He says he's been going to trances recently, then tells me that he went to Nevada last year. Jimmy's stories meld together in a tipsy spiral, but despite his drunken slur and heavy accent, I think I am getting him clearly. When he was in Nevada, they wouldn't let him gamble or drink because he was just 19—though he is 20 now, he points out emphatically—and he tried to gamble anyways but was caught.

"Las Vegas reminds me of Amsterdam," he says. "A place where you can look up, down, left, right, front, behind, but you just go round. Go round. You cannot get out." I nod and agree, though I don't have much frame of reference for his otherworldly stories. While he rolls more cigarettes, he tells me how he left Amsterdam. He didn't have any money, he says, but he had his ticket. The train station he describes sounds like a new annex in Dante's Hell: a crowd pushes and shoves as he makes his way through, people yelling for him to show his ticket. But he tells them he doesn't have one and keeps moving toward the train. "If I show it to someone, they will kick me, take my ticket, and throw me onto the tracks." People grab at him, but he presses through and only when he reaches the train does he finally show his ticket. His voice is triumphant, and I imagine him, inebriated, waving his ticket at the maddened mob from the back of a departing train, people on the platform still clamoring to reach him. A puff of the train's billowing steam mixes with the cigarette smoke escaping his mouth, framing the whole scene.

Jimmy says he was in Amsterdam for New Year's and that it was "the best and the worst New Year's ever. I was out of control." I'm still nodding, saying "Yeah," and thinking about the circular nature of the city, about not being able to get out mentally or physically. Are there cities you cannot escape? I suppose I had thought of Las Vegas that way before, but mostly as a congested pit stop mid-way between my apartment in Utah and my parent's home in Southern California. Perhaps he means he can't escape the memories, and, too quick to judge, I assume he's feeling remorse for riotous living or for enthusiastic pursuits that drive others away, but then he mentions mushrooms and reminds me that they are legal in Amsterdam, and he has friends who can get them. "There are prostitutes shaking behind glass," he says and then giggles, biting his hand to quell the laughter as he looks down at the table.

I ask him why he is in Edinburgh, and he says that he is waiting for a flight. While he waited some girls showed him around town, which is how he got so drunk. He went back to the girls' flat.

"But they were tired," he said, "though I am always disappointed by Scottish girls' flats whether or not I have sex," and he giggles again, still biting his hand. He says he is really funny. I guess he is, though it's hard for me to say if I find him funny or fascinating.

I'm trying hard not to think about him either way because it would mean comparing him to me, which I don't want to do because so many bad study abroad essays make such comparisons in one of two ways: We're different but those differences make us human; or, We're different but when I think about it, we're the same. I know that were I honest with myself, I could probably see that those two sentiments are in fact true, which is why so many boring essays come to such conclusions. But really, Jimmy and I are just two guys up late in a foreign city, not sure what will happen next. We both want bodily comforts we're unlikely to find here in the common room.

All I know of his life is the sex and the drugs and partying, so that's the part that comes through now, his stories of the sensual side of the world, a part I have never given myself permission to explore. I have no idea what he thinks of me. He probably doesn't think of me, which is perhaps the key difference between us. It's just my obsessive nature again, trying to see what can't be seen that makes my thoughts circle around him, filling in gaps for him where I am too shy to ask.

That, of course, was part of the problem with Kirsten. She asked, she prodded. I opened up, as much as I thought I could, more than I had for any other, but it still never felt like there was anything to share, and she took that reticence as distance. I enjoyed my life with her. Life was good. Why add the drama of picking out annoyances? Why worry about the future when it would be as comfortable as the present? This hadn't satisfied her. She worried that I couldn't be supportive, that I'd always be emotionally distant. I told her I was just more comfortable with the quiet, preferred to explore my emotions in writing. I told her I was funny.

JIMMY ASKS IF HE CAN READ what I've been writing, so I hand my journal over to him, and he reads part of this essay, the part about squirrels above.

He asks what "squirrel" is, and I say "écureuil," which, along with *escargot, bonjour* and *hors d'ouvres*, makes up the extent of my French, but he doesn't understand me. He asks if "squirrel" is "*tortue?*" which I think might be a dialect word for squirrel. He waves behind his back and says, "The animal with the big..." I am thinking *tail* but he is thinking *shell*, so I say, "Yeah, a squirrel." And he asks, "Isn't that also called a ... a turtle?" Only then do I recall my limited Spanish, recognizing the similarities between French *tortue* and Spanish *tortuga*. I am sure about *écureuil*, having checked my pronunciation with several French people over the years, but still, I start to doubt. I try drawing a squirrel for him, the quick little line drawing I use for signatures, but he guesses,

"A worm?"

I never was very good at Pictionary.

Luckily, I remember that the common area's bulletin board has a poster with local wildlife on it, so I lead him to it and point out the endangered red squirrel.

"Oh! "*Écureuil!*" he says, repeating back to me what I had said before but in a pronunciation unmistakably more French. The confusion could be blamed on the drink, his limited English, the earliness of the hour, or my mispronunciation of one of the few French words I know.

His reply is nevertheless disheartening: "You understand me, but I don't understand you."

Then, he returns to the table to collect the five rolled smokes and we don't say anything more except "Good night," though it is already morning. Jimmy backs out of the double doors, and I am done writing. It seemed suddenly impossible that anything I might say to anyone would be understood. Breakfast is still several hours away, so I close my journal and head back to bed as the early summer sun begins to rise.

ON RECONSTRUCTION

As the study abroad group piled out of the bus and busied about preparing to hike Helvellyn, a mountain already popular in the days of Wordsworth and Coleridge, I noticed a sign near the trailhead: "Look out for squirrels!"

The sign featured pictures of ruddy, cheery-eyed Eurasian red squirrels and stated that Thirlmere, the forest at the base of Helvellyn, was "one of their last English strongholds." On the map that accompanied the sign, a path branched off the main trail into the heart of the woods. Before we began hiking, I decided that I would leave the group, explore the forest, see a red squirrel, and catch up later. Since this was one of their strongholds, I figured it wouldn't take long.

But when we got to the trail fork, I saw another sign; the Thirlmere trail was closed, "Due to Essential Tree Felling Work." In the distance was a wide, barren dirt road covered in fallen logs; the tractors responsible for the mess were not far ahead. It was difficult to believe that this cutting down would preserve the squirrels' habitat. I stood for several disheartened moments just staring into the forest, apparently one of my last chances to see an English red squirrel, wondering if I should duck under the sign and sneak past the tractors. But I still had another month in the British Isles, and though I'd not seen any in my first month, even in the more likely forests of Scotland, there was still time. At least, that is what I said to comfort myself. This was their last stronghold and our group was slowly making our way south, where the American gray squirrels had invaded and the red squirrels were already extirpated. But my group was making good ground up the mountain, so I shouldered on, cheering myself up by enthusiastically explaining the situation to Pato, the thirteen-year-old son of one of the professors.

I explained what the sign had said: The American gray squirrels were taking over, spreading up from the south of England, and the red squirrels were slowly dying. I also explained what the sign didn't detail: The gray squirrels eat the same foods as the reds but tend to do so earlier in the season, diminishing the supply. I told him about the squirrelpox virus: deadly for the reds, merely annoying for the more robust grays. I told him, and anyone who would listen, that the gray squirrels had been brought to England in 1876 by one Mr. T.U. Brocklehurst, though the problem was substantially increased when the 11th Duke of Bedford, then President of the Zoological Society, liked the animals enough to send living samples throughout England and Ireland to other squirrel enthusiasts. I told Pato that within ten years of a gray squirrel entering a particular forest, all the red squirrels would be dead.

My group found it amusing that I knew all this, but they hadn't come to the United Kingdom for *sciurus vulgaris*. They wanted Romantics, and the plan was to hike over Helvellyn and into Grasmere where we'd visit Wordsworth's two homes, and while we were hiking, we'd quietly pretend we were Coleridge, who had taken this same path and had the same destination in his day. And at the top of Helvellyn, we'd stand at the mountain's pinnacle and look down on majestic, transcendent valleys as a stiff wind battered us and reminded us of the sublime deities of nature. Our windbreakers would protect us and we'd eat trail mix, feeling like we could be anything at all.

THIS WAS BEFORE THE DAYS of ubiquitous cellphones, and because we were hiking through remote areas and mostly staying in country hostels, our study abroad group rarely had internet. I mostly corresponded with Kirsten through postcards and infrequent emails. The infrequency didn't bother me. I'm pragmatic—I wrote when I could and didn't worry about what I could not do. But distance is always harder for the person who stays home, whose life goes on the same but with a big hole to fill, so I knew Kirsten missed me more than I missed her.

In the conversation we'd had just before breaking up, sitting on the concrete steps of my condo, lit by my porch light, she'd said she knew I liked her, but she didn't think I *needed* her. I was unfeeling, like a still pond, she said, with no ripples at all because it remained untouched. There were no signs of affection, she said, other than the postcards I sent her weekly despite living mere blocks from each other.

But I did like her, I liked her very much. I told her that I only invited people in that I trusted. I pointed out all the cooking I'd done for her, a small thing, but something I didn't do for anyone else. I told her I also endured conversations like the one we were having right then, when we talked about how we felt even though I never paid much attention to what was under the surface, not in the moment anyway, preferring Wordsworth's approach, emotion tranquilly recalled from a distance. Kirsten liked to take feelings head on, talking her way to a conclusion.

I worried that the two disparate approaches could never speak to each other, especially since my unflappability was a favorite feature of mine. Engaging in the dialogue she needed for her emotional process felt like betraying my vision of myself.

She said she didn't know if I could really support her emotionally. And, anxious that this was probably true, I suggested we should just call it off.

But I knew that the glassy surface of my emotions was not the same as emotional detachment. I also knew that when I came back from England, I still wanted her in my life. So, days before I left, when we got back together, frozen yogurt in hand, licking spoons, I promised her that if she could learn to worry less about my imperturbability, I could learn to be affectionate enough for her not to worry.

THE PREVIOUS DECEMBER, on the night of my birthday and into the next morning, the historic Provo Tabernacle burned down, the result of aging electrical wires in the attic. I saw the smoke and the helicopters as I dressed in the morning, and, having missed the bus, I walked past the burning wreckage on my way to campus.

That night, Kirsten and I visited the still-glowing embers of the fallen walls, setting up my tripod and camera to capture the gothic building's fiery innards. The park around the tabernacle was covered in fresh snow, and the water from the firehoses had left dangerous icicles every-where. The whole scene depicted a carnage of fire and ice.

This building had represented, in numerous ways, the things we'd enjoyed in our still-recent relationship and dating life. It sat prominently downtown, a midpoint between our two apartments, and we'd walked past it or through its surrounding park as we'd visited each other. On Friday nights, strolling the public galleries, we'd seen the Tabernacle's glowing stained glass. When we'd tried the new hipster restaurants that were blossoming on Center Street, we'd eaten our finds from compostable take-out containers in the green of its landscaping. We'd attended devotionals, choir concerts, art shows, and civic events inside the Tabernacle, but now a fire was taking all that from us. Where a live Nativity had been set up the previous year, bare bushes sagged under the weight of fire-hose ice. The carved Sego lilies that had decorated the pulpit, designs I'd traced over and over with my eyes as we'd sat in the pews, were already ashes. Most of the stained-glass windows were in shards in the freezing mud, now separated from the rest of the park by a chain-link fence.

I don't remember what we argued about the night of the fire, but as I took pictures, neither of us was particularly happy with the other. Once again, it was a question of separation.

I was flying home for the holidays in the morning. This would be our first time spent apart, having only dated about two months. As usual, I was fine with the time apart, knowing there would be Skype and instant messages and phone calls and our signature postcards. Kirsten didn't appreciate the pragmatism, but the newness of the relationship made those feelings difficult to share. She kept silent, and I resented what I felt was her pulling away. Instead, I quietly focused my camera on the smoldering.

WHEN OUR STUDY ABROAD GROUP toured Wordsworth's old houses, idyllically christened Dove Cottage and Rydal Mount, we were greeted by buildings that can only be called *houses* in the architectural sense. The places resembled homes but were really museums of homes. The tour guides and plaques led us through displays of chairs, desks, washing basins, watches, stationary sets. The thesis of each museum was no more complex than "He touched this," sometimes even as feeble as, "He touched something like this time-period appropriate item, but this is not the one."

And yet, the allure of these accumulations is enough to sustain the Wordsworth Trust, the writers in residence who crept behind the scenes, the gift shops and memorial plaques, and the building of extra rooms to house the documents, artifacts, and memorabilia that wouldn't fit neatly into the re-created homes. Enough for glass cases and roped-off rooms. To support this re-creation, other layers of history were scrubbed away or tucked neatly in footnotes: Thomas de Quincy, also a successful writer of the time, purchased Dove Cottage from the Wordsworths and lived there longer, but this will always be Wordsworth's home. Rydal Mount still has a portrait of the great-granddaughter who eventually restored it, but there's no other trace of the people who lived there before and after the Great Poet. The other occupants, the neighbors, those who raised sheep and wrote no words worth remembering, are honored only through the crumbling gravestones in the heavenly cemeteries that dot the countryside. Their markers read "Sacred to the Memory of," but their names are frequently illegible.

ON OUR SECOND FULL DAY in the Lake District, we enjoyed some time off from the group, and I found a launderette with free Wi-Fi; luckily Kirsten was online. We typed back and forth briefly on Google Hangouts while my clothes tumbled. I told her my feet were tired from hiking and that I still hadn't seen any red squirrels, but I told her there were supposed to be some in the Lake District, so I maintained my hope of seeing one.

She told me her roommate was trying to find her a date so they could all go to the First Friday gallery stroll together and then play *Pegs and Jokers*, a game that requires pairs. No one suitable could be found. "It sort of feels like you don't exist anymore," Kirsten typed to me just minutes before the launderette closed and we parted ways. "But I'm glad you're having a great time."

Perhaps because if I had said such a thing, I would have been mostly joking, I tried to assume she was being dramatic for the first point, sincere on the second. As I closed the laptop and bundled up my things, I didn't think anything of the fact that I'd not said anything to contradict her.

MY HOPE OF SEEING A RED SQUIRREL often flamed. Everywhere we looked in the Lake District I saw evidence of their passing: signs for motorists to slow down when squirrels were present, postcards with ecological facts on the back, little statuettes in cottage gardens, hiking signs that said they were present. But nothing of the squirrels themselves. I wrote Kirsten a note on the back of a squirrel postcard, describing the previous day's hike, and then I spent an hour wandering a small downtown looking for a mailbox, discovering in the process the wonder that is honeycomb ice cream.

On one group hike, which took us from the village center, through the woods, through fields of baby sheep, and to the ancient stone circle Castlerigg, I felt particularly optimistic because of several "Watch for Red Squirrels" signs. As with Helvellyn, I stayed in the back of the group. I paused, listened. Looking upward, seeking the signs I knew to look for: their spherical dreys of leaves, the crumbled remains of seed hulls, their chittering often confused with bird sounds. But nothing. Only signs by roads. Only clay statues. Only breezes in the trees.

A MONTH OR SO AFTER the Provo Tabernacle burned down, I attended a presentation by a community historian who described the Tabernacle's role in the city, its construction by Mormon settlers, and its many structural and decorative changes over the years. While the fate of the building's charred remains hadn't yet been decided by Church leaders, the question of preservation was clearly on everyone's mind, and the presenter's main point was that if the building was to be restored to its "historic" image, there would be a wide selection of images to choose from, as the building had changed and evolved with the needs of the people using it.

The historian showed pictures of the original building from the late 1800s, which, in addition to the four corner turrets, had a large central spire. The central tower proved too heavy for the structure, so it was removed not many years after the building's completion. The historian noted that modern building techniques could support the central tower, but she wondered if renovators would include it since no one living remembered the building that way. That point struck me, and I couldn't decide which I would prefer. On the one hand, there was the opportunity to make the Tabernacle look as the first architects had intended, that fifth central tower making an already impressive structure that much more regal and commanding. But then again, how strange the building would appear with an additional tower; the original architects must have felt a similar incongruity when they removed it.

WHEN KIRSTEN AND I broke up that week, I didn't tell anyone, even my younger brother with whom I shared a condo. Of course, she'd told all of her friends and family already, had gotten counsel and comfort from them. When I went to the Natural History Museum with a large group of my friends, I just told them Kirsten couldn't make it, proving her right, that I was too inward for such connections. No need to ripple the pond by sharing my discomfort, perhaps even grief. My friends and family would figure it out eventually when she stopped coming around. I figured I would get used to the discomfort, as I had always done with such things, waiting out the problems until they were not problems anymore.

But her absence felt like a shadow of my real life. Unlike other break-ups, where I had always felt some amount of relief, this separation didn't feel like it could last, which is how I realized that I didn't want it to. So, in a way, it was my own reluctance to tell anyone, my growing discomfort with the thought of us apart, that made me realize I had to fix what I'd done.

AS WE HIKED HELVELLYN, Pato asked why they didn't just let the gray squirrels have the land, since they were more adapted to it. "They should just move the red squirrels somewhere else," he said.

How to counter such logic? Obviously, we see the folly of bringing the gray squirrels to England now, but why is it a problem? Why is one squirrel better than another? There are ecological implications, to be sure—red squirrels are one piece in a puzzle of the forest, helping trees profligate, giving meals to predators, etc. Gray squirrels can do some of these, but they change the local ecologies. And some have suggested moving the reds, perhaps to the Isle of Mann, where there are no greys, but this would disturb the fragile puffin populations, always a ripple when you muck around—but these reasons are rarely mentioned in the popular literature. It is English heritage that gets mentioned most. The red squirrels are part of England's image of itself. Every red squirrel is Beatrix Potter's Squirrel Nutkin. Every squirrel is the one carved into the Ruthwell Cross, which itself was broken and battered then reconstructed. Every squirrel is a descendant of Ratatoskr, revered in England's pagan days.

HALFWAY THROUGH MY STUDY ABROAD, I received this email from Kirsten:

> *This isn't the kind of email you want to get while you are in England...but I just need to explain how I've been feeling about things since you left...*

I felt my chest tighten as I read, crouched at the computer in the common room of a hostel in the woods. A number of worries crossed my mind, but that someone had died flashed prominently. In some ways, the following lines were a relief:

> *I was shocked when you wanted to get back together and really happy because I didn't want us to end. That being said, I guess I'm sort of unclear on why we got back together (besides that I really like you and you seem to like me too and we both seemed less happy without the other one.)*

What I mean is that I don't know if my concerns about you actually being attached to me or wanting to be attached are resolved in my mind...

She went on to say my postcards had gotten less affectionate and were now more like blog posts—all news and happenings, nothing cute or romantic.

Kirsten's email was the first time she'd really hurt or offended me. My emotional distance makes me hard to bruise, but the only thing I saw in the email was ungratefulness, an unwillingness to acknowledge my efforts at affection. I cried on a bus thinking about her email, looking out at the British landscape, seeing only the gray clouds low in the trees. I didn't respond for over a week, though we had internet. I realize now she must have been anxiously waiting for my reply, but I couldn't have responded sooner without clumsily thrashing about, damaging our tenuous relationship. I bought post cards but didn't send them. I kept thinking, "How could people who so thoroughly misunderstand each other have any future together?" But that wasn't really what I was asking myself, it was just a question to the rain beading the bus windows.

AT THE SAME TIME THAT COLONIZERS were reattaching the world's animal populations to new locales, bringing rabbits to Australia, snakes and mongooses to Hawaii, starlings to America, gray squirrels to England, Darwin was teaching about evolution, about the nature of change and survival of the fittest. We understand his theories even better now, about species changing and adapting as populations move across the globe and that even the continents are ever shifting. Evidence suggests that even the red squirrel's ancestors may have come from America first, when the world was colder, the land closer together. Nature is dispassionate about the results: if the red squirrel were given the chance to re-colonize America, they would, but oceans stand in the way now. The gray squirrels wouldn't have been able to accomplish it except they had humans with boats, a resource not to be underestimated. However, the tides have changed. We're repentant of our mistakes and the red squirrels have our sympathies now.

In one nature center, I asked a forest worker what they were doing to preserve the red squirrels in the area, and she mentioned "species control." When I asked what that meant, she got a little squeamish. Guessing at her meaning, I asked "Do you mean killing the grays?"

"We don't like saying it like that," she replied. "There are lots of people who aren't comfortable with that." So yes, they kill the grays in favor of the reds because the reds belong. They are the original. They have a place on the pedestal.

THOUGH I WOULDN'T HAVE SEEN this in myself at the time, I recognize now that my reluctance to feel pain also meant I was reluctant to admit, let alone explain, my own discomfort. I admitted to myself that I was upset and sad at Kirsten's reaction, but I had to convince myself to ask something of her even though correcting someone else's behavior would have felt like I was someone who could be displeased. It was not brave, my eventual reply, but especially as I look back, I see it as an important step in my own emotional landscape, parting the waters to bring up what had been under the surface:

It felt like you acknowledged the things I did for you since I left, said that you loved them, but then said 'But it's not

*enough,' or 'Thanks, but I would have preferred a different
gift instead.' I know that this isn't what you actually meant,
but it is what I first felt, and it hurt.*

Perhaps because I had released the dam at last, other
emotions naturally followed:

*Because, the truth is I can't see a postcard without thinking
of you, and I have made efforts to find postcards I think
you would like, and if my messages were more news than
anything else, it is because I don't see you that often at the
moment and I thought you might like to know what I've
been up to. The cuter messages of the past were sent when
I was seeing you every day. It doesn't make those messages
less true, but it doesn't mean that the update postcards mean
any less. It still means 'Thinking of you pretty much all the
time, and they are happy thoughts.'*

And there in that email, I also told her for the first time
that I loved her: "*Basically, I like you tons. Even love you,
though I am bad at saying it in ways you find meaningful.*"
I signed that email "*Love,*" which I'd never done before.
I had never told any girl I'd loved her.

My mind was scrambling, frantic and hopeful at the
same time. I had the notion that, having said how I felt,
I was prepared to have said my last and be done with it
all. If my feelings were met with more reluctance, there
was nothing else to give.

On paid Wi-Fi, I signed off, with no time or money to
linger for the reply that might settle it, settle me.

AT THE PRESENTATION ABOUT the Provo Tabernacle, the
presenter asked: If the building were to be restored, would
the inside's color scheme resemble the garish blue, orange,

and red that suited the 1890s builders' sensibilities, or would we return to the conservative whitewash, added in the 1950s, or, perhaps have the sea-foam green which the renovators of the 1990s inaccurately thought was fitting of a historical look? There is no one answer to the question of restoration. When one seeks to preserve and to reconstruct, one must pick and choose from a history that was never fixed, was always in flux.

IN GRASMERE, ON A WALK to the hostel from some museum or church or such, a few of us lagged behind on the trail, reveling in the green of the grass, the blue of the flowers that grew under mossy trees and saw the flurry of movement and heard the chittering of what could only be a squirrel. Excited, I hurried to the tree in question, a large, bare oak standing on a gravel path winding its way along Grasmere Lake.

But it was a gray squirrel, not a red, and it felt like an ill omen, a sure sign of the end. The rest of my friends continued on, still laughing, even pausing to dip in the chilly water, but I dragged my feet, feeling as though the appearance of the gray were a personal injury.

FOR WORDSWORTH'S HOMES, the endings have already come in perpetuity. Despite the revolving nature of the estates' residency programs, despite their lived-in qualities, they are static. Endowments and trusts ensure that Wordsworth's bathroom washstand will rest on display so long as England holds. In this, there is consistency, there is knowledge for generations to come; there is a reminder that poetry is a national treasure. In these museums, England identifies its story and tells the story of its identity. Like all things, such tellings will shift over the years, but it will be a slow change, as fixed as each piece is behind glass on the shores of still lakes.

The Tabernacle will be rebuilt, but only in a semblance of its original image, not like a phoenix rising, exactly, because it is transcending its original purpose. A few months after my return from England, the Church decreed that the Tabernacle would become a temple, the most sacred of Mormon buildings, the holy of holies. The Tabernacle will no longer be a space for community gatherings, no more musicals, no more congregational sermons, no more high school or university graduations. Now it will be for sealings, for washings and anointings, for receiving the sacred endowment, a ceremony that prepares believers to pass the sentinels that guard heaven's gates. With the view that these are the solemnest ordinances of the Mormon faith, to become a temple is the highest honor a building might receive, and so, every care was taken in its reconstruction. The architects have restored the central tower. During excavations, workers discovered a painted plaster design for the walls, long forgotten. Those designs are now repeated throughout parts of the temple, like the bride's dressing room, a room the original Tabernacle never had. A fire-scorched painting of Christ from the original Tabernacle is hung with pride, a reminder of the building's past.

FOR THE RED SQUIRRELS, THE FUTURE is still uncertain. By uncertain, I mean I do not think they will survive long in the British wilds. As of 2019, the National Trust is projecting that there will be no red squirrels left in England in ten years, only slightly longer for the British

Isles in general. The gray squirrels are winning, there's no getting rid of them, no matter how much "species control" we carry out. We're just too far behind. The red squirrels' retreats are depleting, losing ground. The strongholds are falling. The farther south you go in England, the less likely you'll see a red squirrel, and the cuter the grey squirrels seem. We know from fossil records that no species lasts forever. But we panic when the world evidences that she is changing yet again. Species disappear while others dangerously flourish, and we ask ourselves, "Did we do this?"

And for all that, we've not given up hope. Volunteers and community programs abound, with annual squirrel counts and gray squirrel hunts. Some forests have even seen the reds' return or their numbers grow. But, if we're honest, the situation is perilous.

I STILL HADN'T SEEN A SQUIRREL when I finally received Kirsten's reply, which I noticed she'd sent just minutes after I'd logged off, but I'd been away from the internet for several days. She responded graciously. She apologized. She said she was grateful for my response. In answer to my promise of more affection, she promised more gratitude. She closed by saying, "I don't want to lose you." And our email chain became less tense, with detailed plans for the rest of the summer: reunions with friends, a Decemberists' concert, grilling, art strolls. Through the emails, our relationship gained strength and a new shape.

The apology meant everything to me. I did not then and I do not now wish to suggest her apparent ingratitude, born of uncertainty, was an excuse for my own distance, I suggest only that this exchange, carried out across vast waters, signaled in both of us a willingness to break something of ourselves, to let crumble the walls that kept each of us from reconstructing a new, united vision. I had to give up the safety I felt in my placid life, where I was comfortable and certain, where I had time to observe and reflect.

I still miss that individuality sometimes. But once you've attached yourself to someone, once you've opened up, let the fires of forgiveness gut you, there will be pieces missing and there will be new, flame-forged, smoldered bits you hadn't known about before. In that moment of reading her email—perhaps it had come even earlier than that, when I'd first written my reply, recognizing that I would never be rid of my weakness so there was no need to hide behind it—I could see my own future, and though Kirsten will later tell me that she still felt doubt and still didn't know what sort of relationship we'd have when I returned, I knew we would at least have one.

EVENTUALLY, I DID SEE A RED SQUIRREL, on the Isle of Wight, where isolation and fierce preservation techniques mean the gray squirrels can't approach. The grays still try to get on the boats that come from the mainland, but the humans on these boats are wiser than their ancestors. The Isle's laws dictate that any boat found to have a gray squirrel on it must return to port (though the head squirrel conservationist there did confide to me that this hasn't happened since the '70s.)

I spent four solitary hours wandering through a small woodland preserve where the reds were supposed to live. I waited patiently in the blinds; I ditched the trails to step gingerly under pines, gazing up for dreys, seeing plenty, finding the tell-tale signs of chewed-out pinecones, but for so long, there was no squirrel. Then, my time running short, I knelt in the forest and prayed to the God of Fallen Sparrows, who, for reasons I don't understand, answered this prayer, and there, almost immediately, was a squirrel crossing the path. I followed it, in awe of the auburn color. A solitary, precarious flame in the blaze of the cool forest.

The cynics (and I count myself among them most days) might question why a god would choose to answer this prayer, such an insignificant request when so many greater problems call for answers, so many other prayers prayed with more faith, more earnestness, more immediacy. I can't say—maybe there is no god who answers prayers, and it was merely a coincidence—but perhaps this was the last chance for a sign, an omen of things at rest. Here, momentarily at least, nothing in my world was out of place.

WHEN THE STUDY ABROAD GROUP arrived in London, I stopped looking for squirrels and instead shopped Portobello Road for rings, and some months later, seated next to each other as husband and wife, Kirsten and I attended the groundbreaking ceremony for the Tabernacle's reconstruction.

DEATH, FIREBIRD

In August of 1998, about to become a high school fresh-man and the hot Arizona sun belting down, I stepped for the first time onto the marching field (non-band nerds might call it the football field). I knew very little about marching band, but since I'd enjoyed middle school band, my parents encouraged me to continue into high school. My first lesson: keep the baritone's mouthpiece out of the sun. I'd burned my lips after letting it sit uncovered on the sidelines for a few minutes. My second lesson: With your full attention focused on staying in step, forming your lips' aperture just so, fingering the keys, finding the next posi-tion on the field, keeping your eye on the drum major, and pointing your horn up, you could forget nearly anything.

I wanted to forget that while I was at band camp and in the first weeks of high school, while I spent my mornings on the field, my days in classrooms, and evenings again on the field carrying out the typical life of a teenager, my mother was at home, finally succumbing to years of cancer.

WHAT I WANTED THEN TO FORGET, I essay now to remember. To solidify what remains. My mother died in September. She slipped into a coma on a Wednesday afternoon and died Friday morning. I had been in high school for only a month, which I mention for two reasons: I was awash in the newness of my situation, invigorated with my new schedule, but also to suggest I have lived more of my life without her than with her, especially when you consider the inattentive childhood years and the selfishness of the early teens. This math weighs heavily sometimes. But also, this is just the way things always were, always will be. When people ask about my mother, I usually start by saying she was quiet and creative, that she had eight children, of which I am the seventh. But ultimately, her early end. Death has become my mother's most distinguishing feature.

A MEMORY:

At high school registration, she and I perused the cafeteria's rows of booths and stations with pamphlets, sign-up sheets, and tired teachers. I had, apparently, taken an exam that had not placed me into Honors English. But my mother insisted I was qualified for it. The beleaguered teacher looked at her notes and shook her head. I had not passed the test. My mother continued to insist. Finally, rolling her eyes, the teacher looked at me and asked:

"How many words do you need to spell *a lot*?"

I looked at my mom, her mahogany-dyed, loosely permed hair bouncing as she nodded slightly, looking at me with her pale, freckled face and kind eyes, whose color I do not recall. Everything about my mother had prepared me for this event. She had drilled into me a respect for grammar, entire lessons delivered in mock questions: "Was she *all like* or just a *little like*?" she'd frequently asked me after my California inflection offended her grammatical sensibilities.

I didn't even have to think, "Two," I replied to the teacher. Only people with less diligent mothers ever wrote *alot*.

The woman *harrumph*-ed and admitted me into the Honors English program. We collected the course books and I read *Of Mice and Men* in its entirety that afternoon, which was perhaps the more accurate test.

IN SUCH A MEMORY, my mother is whole and complete, as she was: strong, determined, solid. She was the mother who loved me, who had my interest at heart. She was also the type of woman who sent a cold burrito back to a restaurant kitchen three times until it returned the perfect temperature; she bought bags of Sun Chips only for herself, the single snack she reserved apart in a pantry frequently ravished by her horde of children. She returned to teachers their notes home with policy suggestions and punctuation corrections in red ink.

I didn't know how much energy this strength took or how often she spent the days in bed so as to have an hour to spend on us.

WHEN YOU HAVE LOST A PARENT, it is sometimes tempting to feel you've been abandoned. Over the years I've frequently felt it was *unfair* that she hadn't attended my high school graduation, unfair that she hadn't been there to welcome me home from my missionary service, unfair she hadn't welcomed my bride with open arms. Those moments of self-pity are often followed by guilt: it is equally unfair of me to want such things, to demand of her more than she could give. Life is what it is, I have told myself on so many occasions. There is no use wanting what you have not been offered.

BUT I ALSO REMEMBER THIS from that first month of school:

One afternoon, as I returned home from school, the house was brightly silent. I dared not make a sound, fearful of disturbing the unexpected and holy reverence suffusing our home. I left my backpack at the door and removed my shoes as though entering a temple.

The sun shone through the upstairs windows on the west side of the house, letting in an intense, warm glow that bounced off every white wall. I passed through the sunbeam, momentarily set ablaze as I ascended the stairs and slowly opened the door to the master suite.

She slept at the bed's edge, awash in that hallowed light, no blanket, her hands under her head and her feet bare. It was possible, with such a glow, to imagine she was well, simply napping. I closed the door, comforted by her very presence. Then, just as suddenly as *relief* washed over me, I realized relief was exactly what I would lose when she was gone.

The memory's emotions still mix. My whole body relaxed with the lightness of the scene, this feeling that everything was as it should be, but also the impending doom, knowing that this feeling would end. There wasn't sadness, though, not exactly. There was the urgency to enjoy the feeling as it was while also recognizing how lucky I had been to experience it, however briefly.

OUR MARCHING BAND SHOW that year was selections from Stravinsky's *Firebird Suite*. I am listening to it now as I type—not the simplified versions adapted for high school marching bands, but the smooth, confident 1919 recording from the New York Philharmonic.

The *Finale* starts soft and sweet, earnest. In our high school arrangement, a trumpet solo accompanied by woodwinds and a xylophone steadily crescendoed to a dramatic trumpet and horn fanfare with the full brass section. The ending's long, bold notes came from all the brass and bass drums clanging like church bells.

As the fanfare reached its climax, we formed a giant firebird, its wingspan from twenty-five-yard line to twenty-five-yard line. I was positioned on the underside of the right wing, just where the wing and body connected. After holding the bird formation for a few bars, we transitioned into a follow-the-leader drill, making the bird pulse with energy as we stepped directly in the path of the person next to us. It was the trick of follow-the-leader drills to blend perfectly with the person before you. This was, really, the trick of all marching bands: to be one, never to draw any attention to oneself, each uniform perfect and crisp and exactly the same. To make a mistake was to mark one's individuality, which everything from the size of the field to the color of the uniforms was designed to prevent. The audience was to see a body but not an individual, and nothing highlighted that more than the large bird flaring across the entire field.

Next, as though reminding us of the firebird's origins and fate, the bird melted toward the home team sideline, losing its feathers and flare as the band formed one long, tight block—a marching band basic, with even lines and even spaces all the way down the field—then, just as we snapped into place, we flanked sharply to the front and marched with the bell tones in a grand company front, a long, bright note hanging in the air as we finished.

THINKING BACK ON THIS TIME just before my mother's end, I assume I must have felt some anxiety, but I don't recall any. In fact, it had seemed to me my mother was going to the doctor less, hadn't gone to the hospital in so long. I didn't realize then that her spending less time in the hospital and receiving hospice care was not a lessening of treatment, not a sign of things going well. But still, her needing medical treatment had been a fact of life for so long. Many people, us children included, didn't see the brunt of it. Only later did my father tell me how hard she tried to hide her pain.

And yet, her illness exuded into so many facets of our home: Many years previous, I had come downstairs in the dark of Christmas morning only to find her, still convalescing from a recent surgery, asleep on the couch. The rummaging through my stocking woke her, and she begged me to return to bed, which I did with a sense of guilt that still haunts the edges of the memory. She ate (which means we did, too) many yellow fruits and vegetables because she'd read they were better at ridding the body of toxins. We talked about her cancer, but we also didn't talk about it; it hovered just beyond each doorway. Or so I recall through the mixed hazes of memory and youth. Though both my parents were often silent about it—my mother out of self-deprecating pride and my father from grief—my dad now tells me that they did discuss it in private. Less than a year earlier, my mother had cried with my dad at a doctor's visit, knowing she'd not be around much longer, and when she'd been asked to volunteer with the women's group at church, my father suggested they find someone else, saying she probably wouldn't survive to Christmas and she wanted the remaining time for her children.

I don't remember feeling so rushed about it, but I do recall one family discussion earlier that year—the topic of conversation suggests I am remembering Easter, but it's entirely possible it was any common Sunday dinner when we sat at the formal table in various stages of our church clothes, when my older siblings came home from college life for dinner and my dad delivered to us his casual and heartfelt sermons, promising us that the things of the soul were "as real to me as breathing." It didn't matter, my dad said that Sunday, if the end was near, we'd all be together again in the Resurrection. He didn't speak in the tones of generic Sunday sermons: he invoked relief from the unimaginable grief he carried with him. We knew the loss he was preparing us for, suggesting a nearness that neither surprised me nor entirely sunk in. I looked at my mother, sitting opposite my father as she always did, together bookending the family they'd made, and she smiled politely at the conversation as though they only mildly concerned her, then leaned over to assist my little brother with something on his plate. Surely, she must have said something, but I recall no words. She had not wanted to have this conversation, my dad told me many years later, but he had insisted they tell us children how little time was left. She let him do the talking.

WHICH IS TO SAY, MY MOTHER could not bring herself to say goodbye.

IN THIS, I TAKE AFTER MY MOTHER. Slinking away, hoping silence will absolve discomfort. Rationalize pain until it is not pain, it is only life, and what is there to do about any of it.

SMALL AS MY WORLD WAS, I had assumed Stravinsky's ballet was the story of the phoenix, the giant bird of Greek myth who died in a wondrous, fiery display to be reborn from the ashes. I also had a significant crush on the X-Men's Jean Grey, aka Phoenix, and had just that summer read the first Harry Potter novel, which features Dumbledore's phoenix companion, Fawkes, so phoenixes were on my mind.

But I was also thinking of life after death. I was taught to believe in a literal resurrection, in glorified bodies of flesh and bone, in families reuniting to live together for eternity. The phoenix was a symbol I was happy to consider, rehearse, and embody on the band field.

But that is not the firebird of the ballet. No, Stravinsky modeled his work on Russian folklore, blending various characters to make a new story. In the ballet, the firebird is a victim of Koschei the Deathless, an immortal sorcerer who has imprisoned many wondrous creatures and thirteen princesses, all rescued by the (charming, I assume) Prince Ivan. After being rescued, the firebird shows Ivan where to find the sorcerer's soul, housed in an egg. The Deathless finally dead, Ivan marries one of the princesses and the tones that ring out in the *Finale* are the celebration of the villain's death, his prisoners' freedom, a wedding.

Still, for me, that final push, those triumphant peals of the bells, will always summon a rising phoenix in a fiery jubilee of new beginnings.

SOMETIME IN EARLY SEPTEMBER, I came home to find Amy, a friend of the family who occasionally sat with my mom, in our front room playing the piano. My mother loved music but never had much talent for it. When she'd been healthy, I'd often come home to find her at the keys slowly plinking out the melody to a favorite hymn. But Amy, a professional musician, sat there now, playing adeptly but reverently, filling the house with music while my mom slept upstairs.

Amy and I had bonded over marching band—in fact, that summer she'd applied to be the band director of my high school, though she hadn't received the position. I gleaned much of my enthusiasm for marching band from her, showed her the music, asked her for advice, and received lessons. A month after my mother's death, on Halloween, when parents usually volunteered at our school's band invitational, she signed up and cheered me on. My dad let her borrow his car to drive me to the event, which I took as a sign of their good will for each other and the main reason I was not at all surprised when they eventually announced their engagement.

MY MOM WENT TO THE HOSPITAL on a Wednesday afternoon. My father told me his last words to her were that he'd see her at the hospital, but she was already in a coma when he arrived. As my mother had requested, they did not try to resuscitate her. She waited in her coma long enough for all eight of her children to arrive from out of town, and then died on Friday morning.

I spent nearly all day Thursday at the hospital, alternating with my siblings sitting near her bedside. At my father's insistence, we each had a private minute alone to say something to her. We were assured, as they do in the movies, that she could hear us. I held her hand, which was warm and smooth, but somehow both rigid and loose at the same time. I had always loved the skin of her hands and arms, always pale but with a blanketing of variegated freckles. I leaned in close to her ear. Like her, I could not bring myself to say goodbye, so in my final moments alone with her, I said nothing until I felt too ashamed of the silence and found the courage only to whisper, *I love you.*

I spent most of the time in the hospital lobby. Not knowing what else to talk about, I chatted with Amy about band and asked her if she would transcribe into my journal her family's recipe for strawberry and cream sheet cake. We all gathered around my mom's bed and sang the hymns she loved. My sister, who had not been to church in years, commented how effortlessly the words of the hymns returned. A nurse asked my dad how long they had been married for, and he replied, "For forever."

Thursday night, I slept at a friend's house, and then my mom died while my friend's dad drove me to the hospital on Friday morning. A few hours after her death, my dad asked what I wanted to do next. I said I wanted to go back to school. I see now that I didn't know how to grieve, or even what to grieve, exactly. We had been expecting this outcome for so long, when it happened, there was a numbness and realization that what I had always known would happen had come to pass. That sense of comfort was gone, but everything else was still there, outside the walls of this dim hospital. Best to resume life, I probably thought.

My father hugged me but, wisely, did not take me to school.

When I did return a week or so later, counselors called me out of class to speak with them in dim offices. I said nothing, mostly shrugging at their questions. I did not know what they wanted to hear. I had shown up for school, what more did they need to know?

I WAS OFTEN ANGRY IN THE WEEKS and months that followed. Being quiet, timid, and a bit of a loner, my anger
mostly came out against my younger brother, the only one
I had any power over. I began to hit him, not hard, but
little smacks and swats when he annoyed me. One day, I
raised my hand in his presence, not even to hit him, and
he flinched away. I recoiled, too. I did not want to be cruel.

That evening as I washed the dishes, I decided that any
issues I saw in his behavior were likely because he was also
grieving, so I would not allow myself to be angry with
him anymore. And if I wasn't going to be angry with him,
the person who annoyed me the most in the world, then
it would be easy not to be angry at anyone. I resolved, as
I wiped a plate dry and set it on the pile next to the sink,
that I would never allow myself to be angry again. I learned
to cast myself into the future, to ask myself: "Will I still
be upset about this tomorrow? Next year? In five years?"
If the answer was "no" to any of these, I didn't need to be
angry now either. I found there was nothing time would
not ease, and so released myself from the present.

It would be many years before I saw that in casting
out my anger, I had dampened my other emotions, too. If
something would not please me in five years, I had trouble
feeling pleased in the moment. But I didn't recognize these
consequences immediately; the awareness came slowly, and
usually with a sense of accomplishment and pride: When
my sophomore literature teacher described existentialism
as "moving aside the curtains of religion and emotion," I
knew what she meant, and when that same year I noticed
an attraction to boys, I decided some feelings were too
troublesome, so I effortlessly and self-righteously arranged
the curtains of my sexuality to avoid social, religious, or

emotional inconvenience; when a church leader called me "emotionally mature," or when an erudite friend claimed I had "an essayist's soul," I congratulated myself for the distance I had achieved from my feelings. I often remembered my decision fondly when I washed dishes by hand. I only began to realize the price I'd paid when my first girlfriend called this same stability "cold-hearted."

I'D LIKE TO SAY I WRITE to reclaim my mother from death, but I know writing my mother does not conjure her, rather, only my fluctuating memory of her. I summon myself. Mark Doty, in his essay "Return to Sender: Memory, Betrayal, and Memoir" says,

> The past is not static, or ever truly complete; as we age we see from new positions, shifting angles. A therapist friend of mine likes to use the metaphor of the kind of spiral stair that winds up inside a lighthouse. As one moves up that stair, the core at the center doesn't change, but one continually sees it from another vantage point; if the past is a core of who we are, then our movement in time always brings us into a new relation to that core.

Which is to say, it is not just memory that is fluid, but the self as well, always progressing. My position relative to the memory has shifted. I worry now that I was indifferent, that I ignored her pain in pursuit of my own sense of normalcy. I see now that I didn't know what else to do. As I type this, I remember a conversation with a friend several months prior, at the very end of middle school. That year, I had joined the drama club and spent many late afternoons in the theater, and one evening I told a friend I loved drama because it kept me away from home.

This is the only memory that suggests I experienced any tension or discomfort before the final loss.

I remember my father rearranging his schedule to see me perform as Fagin in *Oliver Twist*. I don't remember my mother being in the audience, but whether that was because of course she came and her presence wasn't questioned or because she was too ill at home, I don't know. I remember our performances and the rehearsals well, but almost nothing of my mother from those months. Which is all to say, I was thinking of myself then. Now, as an adult sitting alone in front of a computer, trying desperately to recall the sound of my mother's voice as I consider that I feel both grief at her loss and guilt that I did not grieve enough, I wish I could return to shake myself, force myself to see her as she was, to ask her what she cannot now say.

Unless of course, she can speak now. The spirits of the dead, Mormons believe, await resurrection in a Spirit World close to Earth. In the Spirit World, the souls of the righteous are put to work proselytizing unconverted souls, but their duties sometimes allow them to interact with the mortal world. Interactions between spirits and mortals are rare, and often kept private. With the afterlife, I have had only one experience: When I was five, I heard my grandfather singing his favorite hymn at his own funeral. More recently, several members of my family say that my mother has visited them in dreams, even a sister-in-law who never met her in this life. The completionist in me, the essayist grasping after every little thread, is tempted to tell you what my mother said and to whom, but this would be a betrayal. The visitations were shared with me in confidence, in reverence. All I really need say now is that I often wonder, if visitations are something the afterlife allows, why she hasn't visited *me*.

One sibling suggested that my mother, keeping tabs on us all from the other side, isn't worried about me. This, obviously, is unfair.

IF MY LANGUAGE "…Mormons believe…" suggests some hesitancy to personally identify with a belief in the Spirit World, you have read correctly. Do I believe the spirits of the dead wait for us on the other side of the veil? Can my mother see me, even as I type this? Could she really visit me if she saw a true need to? I once would have fervently said, *Yes!*, but now, the most honest answer I can give is, *I hope so.*

ON THE WEDNESDAY SHE WENT into the hospital, I returned home from school to find an ambulance in the driveway. I rushed inside but was almost immediately swept aside by my father so the paramedics could carry her out, strapped to a stretcher with an oxygen mask over her face.

My dad must have said something, but perhaps not. He admits he does not remember that I was there at all, consumed as he was with panic. I don't remember anything else between that moment and the end of band rehearsal that evening, but I imagine I was either fraught with worry and going through the motions of what I thought I should do, or I figured this was just another trip to the hospital—there had already been so many.

Recounting this memory to my father, he apologized for not remembering me then and for being so emotionally absent after, but I hold no grudge against him. He talked then and recalls again now that with my mother's death, he simply wanted to disappear, could not fathom life without her.

OTHERS, ESPECIALLY MY FATHER and my witchy sister-in-law, often invoke my mother's presence. When Kirsten and I married, our fathers sat next to the officiator, as is tradition in Mormon marriages (*sealings*, we call them), and where the mothers usually sit—on either side of the couple to be wed—our step-mothers sat. But after, as he did on the day I went through the temple for the first time, when I returned from my mission, at most every important milestone, he said she was there and that she was proud of me.

I say, *I know*, because I want that to be true, want to think there is a relationship that continues all these years later. But I feel the relationship less and less. Her position is slipping: once "the mother who raised me," increasingly only "the mother who died."

KIRSTEN OFTEN CRIES WHEN WE discuss my mother, saying she wishes she had met her. I also wish I had gotten to know her. I am often envious of my older siblings who had the chance, though brief, to know her as adults, to consult about adult problems and seek adult answers.

But let's be honest: I don't know what my relationship with my mother would be like. So many friends tell me of their strained relationships with their own mothers. It is easy to idolize her through the absences. I like to think we'd chat often, though this would be out of character for both of us, as I call my father perhaps less than once a month and my siblings even less. Some of my siblings I've not had a real conversation with in years.

Sometimes I fear that the part of myself which draws away from others would be fixed (or never broken) had she not left. But I am, in so many ways, her son more than my father's. I was always the one to sit apart, to step back and watch. Not shy, but content to observe without interference.

I HAD A DREAM SHORTLY AFTER my mother's death: An ambulance takes my mother to an open-air hospital on the edge of the Grand Canyon. She is laid out on a stretcher, and my father and other family members hurry after her while white-coated doctors wheel her through various rooms, attaching tubes as they go. The scene is all in stage lighting, no moon or stars clutter the black sky.

I sit on the opposite rim of the canyon, my back to the scene, typing away on my computer. In the dream, I am writing a story about two men in love. I have my own, separate, spotlight.

I awoke thinking I had committed some grave sin, convinced I would be separated from my family in death. Concerned, I asked a religious leader—without telling him the embarrassing details—how to interpret dreams. He said if God meant anything by the dream, he would send an interpretation for it. No suitable interpretation arrived, but all these years later, I am still enacting the dream, as I've reenacted it so many times in so many ways, and I begin to see what it means. My grief lies not in the chasm between me and my mother—there is nothing to be done about the distance. Rather, I grieve that I cannot will my dream self to turn around and see.

SEVERAL MONTHS AFTER HER DEATH, I was sitting in the small passenger seat of my sister's pick-up truck, barely squeezed in the back with the fast-food wrappers and gym clothes cluttering the floor. I saw what looked to be a school assignment, and since my sister majored in creative writing and often wrote interesting stories, I picked it up to read. I did not yet know what a personal essay was, so I was surprised to find a lyrical, melancholy reflection about seeing our mom everywhere, even in the repose of Tucson's enveloping mountains. Feeling like I had invaded some personal moment of grief, I dropped the paper and, characteristically, never spoke to my sister about it.

But I knew what she meant. For years, I saw my mother in others' bodies, especially in crowds. Anytime a middle-aged woman in a modest blouse had her back to me or I saw a volume of dark maroon hair in an early-nineties curl I had a moment of elation until I remembered it could not be her.

Perhaps it is only the change in fashions, but I haven't seen my mother this way in years.

THE LAST NOTES OF *FIREBIRD'S FINALE*, though they are jubilant, will always be the sunrise realization of my mother's death, my waking from a dream to reality. That Wednesday night, we did a full run-through of our show. After the last note finished, I was staring up at the judges' box (what we band nerds called the press box) and my arms were tired from holding up my horn, but my heart was beating with the excitement and energy of a completed set. I released my lips from the mouthpiece, breathing the heavy breaths of fulfillment while trying to hold the rest of my body, still ringing with the final notes, at rigid attention. At the drum major's signal, I lowered my horn, and the instructor said we'd finished for the night. I walked to the sidelines where my large silver case waited and suddenly remembered what I had momentarily been swept away from. When I got to the band room to put my horn away, our neighbor was waiting for me. She'd been asked to drive me to the hospital.

EARLY THAT SAME MORNING, I had thought I was up first. I dressed in my room and moved through the upstairs hall quietly, tracing, as I always did, the circuitous border of the Holbein rug that hung on the wall, then tip-toeing down the stairs. In the kitchen, I finally flipped on the lights, only to hear her groan in the family room. Where the kitchen light just barely reached, she shrank into her pink recliner, wrapped in a robe, her face contorted in pain as her hands white-knuckled the padded arms. Through clenched teeth, she asked me to turn out the lights.

Trying not to disturb her further, I ate my cereal as silently as possible and shuffled through the dark to pack my lunch.

As many who grieve do, I wish I could go back to re-live this scene. Had I known this request for darkness would be her last words to me, I would have written them down verbatim, or better, gone to her side and requested she say something else. It is too much to hope either of us would have said goodbye, but perhaps if I had been more awake, I would have comforted her or woken my father to tend to her. I certainly wouldn't have slouched through the dim house as I did, packing my bookbag as though it were any other day, slipping out the front door unobtrusively, leaving her alone to endure the silence and the dark.

I THOUGHT OF YOU

I sit at my desk to write but must clear a space to work first. Kirsten and I married and moved in together almost two months ago, and our things are still finding their places in the small apartment, plus, my desk is the first solid object encountered as we enter the basement apartment so we tend to pile all the things here. I push aside stacks of mail and homeless knickknacks to open my computer, and as all productive writers do, I go first to Facebook and check my notifications. Two people have sent me squirrel links. My mother-in-law posted a picture of a squirrel eating seeds on her snow-packed deck, and a friend posted a squirrel poised as though on a great journey into the unknown, a wide expanse of a flagstone walkway before her—in both tagged the squirrel with my name.

These squirrel links, via Facebook or email, are typical. Just in the last week, these three others: My brother's wife posted about a British chef who serves gray squirrel pasty as part of red squirrel conservation. A classmate sent me a National Geographic article about a saber-toothed squirrel, probably one of the world's first mammals; it looks uncannily like the squirrel from the *Ice Age* movies—and before I've even had time to revise this essay, another friend has emailed me this same link, "breaking news!" though it's hard to imagine anything urgent about squirrel bones. My wife's aunt linked me to a photo essay of squirrels posing as if they were riding a skateboard, playing the piano, or pushing a wheelchair, with an explanation of the photographer's clever use of peanut butter to encourage interaction with the props. In her comments on the link, the aunt said she hoped I hadn't seen the pictures before, and when I told her that I hadn't, she was genuinely happy—or she at least seemed to be. It is so hard to tell what is genuine or just polite or even ironic over Facebook; a colon and a parenthesis only go so far in conveying the full range of human emotions.

I was happy to report that I had not seen that series before. With the abundance of kitschy squirrel content on the internet, it is rather unusual to get five fresh articles or photos in one week, especially because I get a lot of squirrel links. I mean, I've repeatedly been sent the picture of the giraffe licking the squirrel, the squirrels fighting with lightsabers, the squirrel underpants, the video of the UCLA students helping a small squirrel get over a wall with a backpack, the squirrel running under a race car, and the squirrel passed out with beer. And many people either say they hope I hadn't seen it before, or (often incorrectly) assume I haven't and that I'll be thrilled.

I am thrilled, so I often lie. While the law of diminishing returns requires that the novelty of a waterskiing squirrel wears off over time, I encourage even repeat links because I don't want to dissuade people. I like that they join me in my quirk. I like being thought of.

AND SOMETIMES, SUCH FINDS lead to real gems. For example, while I was in London, a friend asked if I'd seen the squirrel painting on display in the National Gallery. She'd seen it on her visit and thought of me. I asked her more about it: Does it depict a woman holding a squirrel on her lap? Does it have a turquoise background? Is there a starling in the picture? She hadn't paid attention enough to remember all of those details, but when I made my way to the National Gallery, I was not surprised to find that the painting was indeed Hans Holbein the Younger's *A Lady with a Squirrel and a Starling*.

Before you think I'm completely obsessed, I'll assure you that I only learned the name of the painter, the piece's history, and even the title while reading the catalog entry at the museum. The only thing I knew before entering the gallery was that, as far as I can tell, only two famous paintings in the Western canon prominently feature squirrels. (And reader, I would love to be proved wrong if you know of others.)

I have *A Lady with a Squirrel and a Starling* here on my desk with me, somewhere in a pile of books I've been recently re-reading. It is on the cover of Devin Johnston's *Creaturely and Other Essays* that I first saw Holbein's painting. And again, even that book I only found because a friend thought of me: my professor and I were perusing the essay section of the Prairie Lights Bookstore in Iowa City when he noticed *Creaturely*. Knowing I'd be interested in a book with a squirrel on the cover, he pulled it off the shelf and handed it to me. I was of course delighted and bought the copy.

Each of the essays in Johnston's slim volume explores the intersections of urban life, wildlife, and philosophy. I'll rave for a moment to say that the essay on mice ended up being my favorite in the whole book, and, while I'm being honest, that the squirrel essay bored me the first time I read it, though I liked it better the second and third time. Johnston's squirrel essay, titled "Separate Worlds," attempts to understand Jacob von Uexküll's philosophy of *umwelt*, the idea that every person and animal has their own view of the world even when they occupy the same environment. In the umwelt theory, the difference between self and surroundings blurs; the mind can only work with the stimulations it receives from surroundings, and so the surroundings are only perceived in their importance to the self. No wonder, then, that we see faces in the rocks of Martian frontiers, a man in the moon, green men in the knots of tress, the repose of sleeping women in mountain ranges. We are prone, always, to think of ourselves in all we see. No wonder, too, that essayists work associatively, that all they need is the ability to discern the infinite suggestiveness of common things because when we look at the world around us, we see only how it relates to us, which is just one reason it's so flattering to have twice had friends point me toward *A Lady With A Squirrel and a Starling*.

But Holbein's painting of this lady—scholars generally agree that her name is Anne Lovell—is not among his most famous works. More people know his portrait of King Henry VIII or *The Ambassadors*, which famously portrays two men leaning against a table filled with globes, instruments musical and cartographical, and books. These still life items are typical examples of *vanitas*, collected items meant to symbolize the transience of life and the inevitability of death. But this painting is an unusual example of the vanitas because at the ambassadors' feet, in the middle of the picture, is a smudge of paint that when viewed straight on seems like nothing in particular, but when you view the painting from the side morphs into an anatomically correct human skull.

When I first saw *The Ambassadors* in a book of illusions, I thought that it was a joke, i.e., the book had distorted a painting, because why would someone do that, and did people that long ago really have that kind of humor? But when I saw it again in a high school history textbook, I realized it was real. No surprise, then, that I would find this painting repeatedly making appearances in books before seeing it *in galleria*: Wikipedia confirms that this painting is the most famous example of *perspectival anamorphosis*.

The Ambassadors hung in the National Gallery just to the left of Lady Lovell, suspended from the ceiling a foot off the wall so that viewers might more easily see the skull askance, which is what most people come to see.

Even as a young boy looking through illusion books, I focused on the skull, twisting the book to see it and paying no attention to the rich details of the vanitas, such as the meticulously accurate maps or the exhaustive patterns of the two rugs—such rugs are now called *Holbein rugs* because he painted them so frequently and in such detail.—He painted the men's clothing sumptuously, every fold and pleat in place, the velvet as soft on the eyes as real velvet on the fingers, and yet I hardly noticed it for the skull looming obscurely. Nor did the other people I observed looking at the painting in the National Gallery, most of whom barely considered the painting in its entirety before viewing it from the side.

The various books and articles about the painting debate the purpose of the skull—the skull as a symbol is common enough in other paintings of the time, *a memento mori*, a reminder of impending death and hell—but the anamorphosis grabs our attention, and we have to wonder if it is more than just skull qua skull, especially given that you cannot view the skull and the rest of the painting at the same time. You must choose one or the other. If you choose to look at anything besides the skull you must confront the painting straight on, but the smudge on the rug distracts you the whole time so that you are constantly jarred by its unnatural presence, by the way it seems to float over the rest of the painting, the way its amorphic shape clashes with the realistic depiction of the fur-clad ambassadors and their erudite knickknacks. But if you choose to look at the skull, moving to the right of the picture or twisting the book, you lose the rest, and only the skull remains. If you remember death, you must forget life. Some theorize that he painted it this way because the painting was going to hang in a stairway, so people approaching the painting would contemplate their mortality first, see the rest later; others suggest that Holbein was just showing off.

Either way, many critics agree that the painting's clear striation of *vanitas* is meant to represent heaven, earth, and hell, with the top tier of star charts and astrolabes representing heaven, the musical scores and maps connote the terrestrial, and the distorted human skull, hell.

I REALIZE AS I WRITE THIS that I have my own *vanitas* right here on my desk. To the right of my computer screen is a clock, one of the most common *vanitas* in art; next to that, a globe; and tucked under that, an African lion skull, teeth naturally bared. The skull makes a formidable desk ornament, one that gets a lot of attention as guests enter the apartment. I fancy that anyone seeing me sitting here would think of me as a latter-day likeness of late Renaissance art: A scholar at his desk, looking across his small room, time dripping away, the world looming, and mortality a constant presence.

Despite these contemporary *vanitas*, the skull is the only real reminder of death on my desk. But really, the lion skull doesn't remind anyone of their own death, despite its three-inch fangs. The form is too inhuman. If anything on the desk is looming and grim, it is the stack of ungraded papers, the utility bills, and the jury summons. Death is now removed from everyday life, and here in the bustle of Kirsten's and my living room, the skull is as novel as the plastic bobblehead squirrel next to the clock.

With the exception of the clock—a retro-style alarm clock with bells and a little hammer at the top—the others are all gifts, mementos. The lion skull came from my best friend who lived in Africa as a teen; his wife did not like the skull, so he gave it to me. I wasn't married yet, so I had no wife to object, and though Kirsten did object to its display in the front room after our marriage, I eventually convinced her it complements our vintage-clutter decorating scheme. I also have a brick that my freshman roommate acquired from the demolition site of our dorm building, seeing it now, I can almost hear the echoes of the Simon and Garfunkel albums we bonded over. The globe was my wedding gift to Kirsten. Its oceans are black veneer, and each country an inlaid semi-precious stone. Kirsten collects maps, so any interesting map or globe I see reminds me of her. Her wedding gift to me, a leather messenger bag, follows me nearly everywhere and presently rests at the foot of the desk.

And in marriage, our other *vanitas* have begun to mingle, too. Notably, the journals and keepsakes we've accumulated since childhood. For convenience, but mostly driven by a lack of space, we spent an afternoon combing through yearbooks and scrapbooks, consolidating our pasts into a shared storage box. Our memories are now as linked as the present moment.

FINDING SOUVENIRS FOR EACH OTHER was an early staple of our relationship. Just a few weeks after our first dates, I was on my way to a conference in Iowa (the same one that found me and my professor in the bookstore) and I promised Kirsten that I'd send her a postcard. She said she actually loved post cards, collected them. So, I searched the conference hall for every postcard I could find and mailed them all to her. When she traveled to Seattle for a friend's wedding, she returned with a squirrel puppet. When she went to Guatemala, she gifted me a giant acorn.

Kirsten is a collector, making it easy to find souvenirs she'd love: In every book store, thrift shop, or antique dealer, I browse for old maps and blue and white plates. I have channeled my own enthusiasm into her collections, looking everywhere for souvenirs, even when I am only gone for an afternoon.

SOUVENIRS, LITERALLY "MEMORY," or "to come to mind," are common enough gifts, but I always feel odd about them when I am on a trip, or when others bring them to me. What are you to remember from the gifts I might buy? Am I to celebrate your travels? While I swear I'm not still bitter about the t-shirt reading "My parents went to Hawaii and all I got was this lousy t-shirt," I'll bring it up to suggest that much of the kitsch we cart around the world is quite useless, meant to momentarily amuse but mostly to suggest we owe those we leave behind some gift upon our return. I don't begrudge you your collection of key chains, magnets, etc, but without an interest in those items or the places you visited, I have no need for them. This is not to say I wouldn't love a gift (when in doubt, bring chocolate), only that I feel a certain distrust of prepackaged souvenirs in museum shops. Torn as I am by the desire to please and my Scrooge-ish nature, I set the impossible standard for myself of finding only natural souvenirs, ones not from gift shops, ones I think you will like, not just ones I thought were novel. But the best souvenirs, besides being unique, spark joy in the giver, as well. They know the receiver well enough to know what they love and so they see their lover in every perfect gift. Which is how every map, every postcard, every blue and white plate has become *memento Kirsten.*

So, of course, every squirrel becomes *memento skoticus* for those who know me. That's where the bobblehead squirrel on my desk came from: Kirsten's aunt returned from a vacation to Seattle and brought us the squirrel as a small thank-you for house sitting.

On the car ride home, I apologized to Kirsten about the squirrel, suggesting she should probably get used to such presents because once someone knows I like squirrels, that's all they get me, and since we were linked now, she was in on the squirrel thing, too.

That same day, Kirsten told her mother over the phone that she was going to send a gift list for our birthdays and Christmas, as her mom had requested. Her mom said "Well, I already got you some stuff. I got Scott something with a squirrel—" but then Kirsten cut her off since I could hear their conversation on the speakerphone. It wasn't really a surprise, though, it's what happens for

Christmas and my birthday, and really the rest of the year. (If you're curious, she got me a set of novelty whisks with squirrel-shaped wires, the same gift I received from my step-mom that year, and when I shared pictures after Christmas, Kirsten's step-mom said she had almost bought them for me, as well.)

Such is the life of an enthusiast: Take a quick walk around the living room/kitchen area and you'll encounter all manner of gifts received: a small stone squirrel from my mother-in-law; a squirrel-shaped crystal candy dish from Kirsten's grandma; a sign that says, "Beware of Attack Squirrel," from my brother; a throw blanket with a squirrel stitched in the corner from Kirsten last Christmas; a stuffed animal squirrel from my lion-skull friend's mother; a hand towel with a squirrel playing the drums from a former roommate; a small porcelain squirrel, yet another friend; and now, my two new squirrel-shaped whisks. There is more in the bedroom, yet more in storage boxes.

"I saw a squirrel and I thought of you," they say.

"I THOUGHT OF YOU" IS, perhaps, one of the most confounding sentences in our language. It is focused on the self, I. I thought. I did something. I saw. I went. But, amidst all that, I thought of you. It ends with *you*. I set aside my own life, my own thoughts. Whatever I was doing is now less important, and you are now present in the umwelt of my life. The sphere I've created for myself touches yours. The more trivial the catalyst, the greater the compliment.

"I thought of you" is different from "You were on my mind." The latter implies brooding and regret, of weight pressing down. You were with me because you are in pain and I am praying for you. You were pressing on my broken heart. You were in the back whispering and I couldn't concentrate. It is the twisted skull made true. It is hell and death at the cost of life.

And though "I thought of you" is fleeting and momentary like a squirrel leaping in overhead boughs, it is joyful. There is a smile implied.

AN HOUR OR SO AFTER I'D DRAFTED the section above, my friend tagged me on Facebook:

> I'm grading portfolios right now, and I just discovered that one of my students wrote a personal essay entitled "Squirrel." And I thought of you.

THE OTHER FAMOUS SQUIRREL PAINTING (you might recall some fifty pages ago when I said there are two) is John Singleton Copley's *Boy with a Squirrel*, which depicts the young Henry Pelham (Copley's half-brother) with a flying squirrel on a chain leash. This was the first famous American painting, the piece that got Copley the attention of British art patrons, the one by which Copley achieved a name and fame. He would go on to paint portraits of the colonial elite, then move to Europe to paint famous battles. But he started his fame with a picture of his brother and a pet squirrel. The portrait made its way to London via a sea captain who promised to show it to a painter friend who then showed it to another painter, Sir Joshua Reynolds, who decided to display it at the Society of Artists in London. By that time the sea captain had sailed again; he'd forgotten to say who had created the painting, a problem since anonymous work could not be displayed at the Society. Luckily, a sailor recognized Copley's hand. (Copley lived on the Wharf, and his mother was a favorite tobacconist of sailors'.) Even then, when the piece was finally displayed it was displayed erroneously under the name William Copley.

You will find no *vanitas* in Copley's work, at least not ones recognizable by Holbein's standards. Of course, Copley painted his pictures some two hundred years after Holbein, and the Dutch Renaissance styles were now passé. But another reason that you will not find the symbols of the old world, that Copley's first paintings seem both rough and uniquely styled, was that he had never seen a masterpiece painting. In colonial Boston, all that he had access to were portraits painted by local artists less skilled than himself and rough replicas of classics that an art teacher had brought from Europe. Only when Copley's fame in London gave him funds to travel to Europe did he finally get to study the masterpieces that were most artists' first texts. He described the old replications as crude, and the original paintings as seeing for the first time.

He went on to paint grand scenes of violence and war in the English tradition, but his portraiture remained grounded in an American roughness, realism with an optimistic glow. But there are still *mementos* in Copley's work, *memento Americana*. Samuel Adams's portrait is stern, and he points defiantly at a mandate from the king, his own documents of independence also present. Paul Revere sits contemplatively, with the tools of his trade in hand, a silver teapot and silversmithing instruments. Other portraits show books, John Hancock with his pen in hand and a book in front of him, as though ready to scratch out his famous signature. There are flowers and newspapers, dolls and grapes. These are the strength of America, its willfulness in youth and independence, its wealth and abundance, its intelligence. And, of course, you will see the squirrel, its chain golden, water and food at the ready. American abundance, food for sustenance. The wilderness, represented by the squirrel, is tamed, chained, and captivated. That which we feared is festive and fruit-ful. Even in Copley's portrait of his own family, we see a scene of abundance and wealth, curtains and drapes not quite concealing a landscape in the background, wild but framed by civilization.

Looking closely, you will notice that Lady Lovell's squirrel in Holbein's painting is also chained. I suppose in real life chains would be necessary to keep a squir-rel in place, but most scholars agree that Holbein didn't pose Lady Lovell with an actual squirrel in her lap, that he painted it on afterward to represent the family crest, which shows three squirrels, a chevron through the middle on a yellow field. I actually saw this crest while touring Middle Temple Hall in London—just two streets over from Charles Lamb's old haunts—though I didn't know at the time what family it belonged to. It was only while I was researching "squirrel" and "Lovell" that I found an 1880 address from Mr. Harvie-Brown, a naturalist in Scotland discussing the use of squirrels in coats of arms, and I made the connection. There is nothing on the crest I saw in Middle Temple that indicates the Lovell family specifically, other than the squirrels and chevron. The text, though Latin and abbreviated, doesn't say *Lovell* anywhere, though it does have *Ranulph*. That *Lovell* and *Ranulph* both mean *Wolf* seems an uncanny coincidence more than any real connection. Also in that same naturalist address, I found a passage about caged squirrels being hung outside shops, to act as living signs, a passage from Charles Lamb's

1825 sketch "In Re Squirrels," which Mr. Harvie-Brown quoted without citing:

> *What is gone with the Cages with the climbing Squirrel and bells to them, which were formerly the indispensable appendage to the outside of a Tinman's shop, and were in fact the only Live Signs?*

Why the need to cage and chain the squirrel? Mr. Harvie-Brown suggests that squirrel hunting in England began as a symbol of Christian dominance since the red squirrel in Norse mythology is a prominent figure of the World Tree, scurrying between Heaven, Earth, and Hell, sowing discord. Perhaps the fully Christianized English— and their colonial counterparts—still held traces of that pagan fear, such that they were comfortable taming such wildness, but never fully trusting it. The squirrel, after all, is one of the most adaptable animals. It thrives in the forests with the rest of the beasts, but it also makes its home in our cities, in our attics, and in our backyard trees. For those looking for symbols, for reminders and mementos, the squirrel reminds us that we have never really gained control, never conquered nature. In art history we learn that the English and colonists did indeed have a distrust of the untamed wilderness, and so landscape painting almost always had a human element to it: a fence, a railroad, a cottage. Anything wild and untamed was savage and pagan, the realm of witches and heathens, where death roamed unhindered. The only cure for the fear of death was the plow and scythe and chain.

I'D MEANT TO END THE ESSAY THERE, but I realize there is one other *memento mori* on my desk—right between the clock and the globe—which I placed there this weekend because I don't yet have anywhere else to store it. A cute, wooden scarecrow doll that my mom made ages ago, and which I just inherited last week. The scarecrow's shirt is a green wooden T, straw protruding from its sleeves, and two yellow planks of trousers hang from twine loops. The eyes are wide and crossed, the mouth is a wiggle of a smile. It sits on a dowel, suspended in a paper pumpkin patch. Most of the things I inherited from my mom are holiday-related because she sold such decorations at craft fairs, both for profit and pleasure. It's Christmas time as I write this, so the Father Christmas doll at the centerpiece of our dining table and her nativity covering our end table both fit in with the mood of the house; the scarecrow stands out, especially because it doesn't fit our vintage decorating style—it's too cute—but we'll be keeping it anyhow, putting it out for every Halloween and Thanksgiving from here on out, just like my mom did.

All of my siblings received similar decorations; there were plenty of them to spare. She made them *en masse*; all year we'd come home from school and find her at the kitchen table with her craft supplies strewn about. Every September, she made cornhusk witches by the dozen. She sewed adorable quilted jack-o-lanterns that you could also turn around to hide the face to become quilted pumpkins for Thanksgiving, for which she also made quilted turkeys and cornhusk Pilgrims. She made wooden Pilgrims, too, as cute as the scarecrow, with eyes less crossed, but smiles just as wiggling. By the time Halloween had passed, she'd moved on to Christmas: *Nutcracker* ballerinas, glass ornaments, and Father Christmas dolls. Some of these decorations were her own design—she won first place in a craft magazine's design competition for a witch pattern—but most of her crafts were only variations on common crafts. A quick search online will show plenty of cornhusk dolls in the same style as my mom's, and the cute, wooden figures of Pilgrims, witches, scarecrows, etc, I've seen dozens of times in the homes of middle-aged women who decorate with a folksy-cute rustic theme. I know my mom's crafts were not unique in style or form, and I wonder why I even keep them. She may have decorated with them, yes, but in all likelihood, this scarecrow was just an unsold item, or maybe a model for future crafts, or a display for her booth at the craft fair. This scarecrow is not a good representation of her, it is just a part of her memory. Nor is it even specific for me: I got this one because my siblings and I drew lots to decide who got what, and if I remember correctly, these crafts were distributed last, after the things of value, like the wedding china and the rocking chair.

Still, it is hard to throw away these things, things that she made and touched. There is no resemblance between the crooked smile on the scarecrow and my mom's smile, which I only remember because I keep a picture of her and my dad on the magnet board in our kitchen. I took the picture at the party we kids threw for their 25th anniversary, a year before she died. She's wearing a pink blouse with purple butterflies; my dad wears a navy polo. They're standing in the kitchen, plastic cups and dirty dishes on the counter behind them, remnants of the party. And they're smiling, both of them leaning in toward each other.

I've plucked the picture from the kitchen, and it's on my desk now, too, right by the keyboard where I can look at it while I type. And having that smile before me, and the scarecrow next to me, I remember anew those days when

I'd come home from school and she'd made the kitchen table into her pallet of paint and twine, and she would let me brush on eyes or tie ribbons, and she would ask me how my day was, and what I had learned at school. This is where she taught me about her passion for crafts, helped me make my own decorations, my own ornaments for the Christmas tree, which I now think are ugly and resist hanging on the tree but still do every year. Here her hands guided mine, here she taught me what it was to find pleasure in small things, even those that are trivial and quotidian, like holiday decorations and ubiquitous rodents. My mother is years dead by now, but these cheesy decorations, these keepsakes, and these hand-me-down treasures press forward as I think of her. These fragments of lives that clutter my desk are the squirrels that run between life and death, *memento mori* of what has passed, but *memento vivere* of lives lived and yet to be lived.

LIVES YET TO BE LIVED

You and I walk through a late spring forest outside Frankfurt, holding hands and chatting. I look for squirrels and see none, but their absence creates a lingering magic: the possibility of the unseen clings to the hidden side of every mossy trunk. We had not expected to be here, in these German woods, but our flight was canceled, so a layover became a night in the country. We hadn't expected to end up in Kazakhstan, either, but as our year in Central Asia comes to an end, it seemed to have gone by so quickly. We'd wanted adventure: you were tired of teaching in American public schools, and I remained unaccepted to graduate programs, so we'd gone to a place few of our friends had heard of.

Kazakhstan had been the glittering unknown, something apart from the hum-drum routines of home, but now, as we follow the path through German trees, we discuss the anticipated reunion with friends in America. We'll probably never see our Kazakh friends again, we mourn. We consider the long, deep winter we've left behind as I turn my head to follow a promising sound. It's only birdsong. We sit on a bench and listen. *What if we can't have children*, we ask each other.

I HEAR SOMETHING CLATTER, just a scuffling of stones underfoot, and I am reminded of dry beans cast onto *kumalak* fortune-telling tables in a Kazakh market. You were still recovering from the emergency surgery that removed a tumor from your uterus when we walked the streets of Astana during the early springtime Nauruz festival. Old women sat on overturned buckets, spilling and sorting red beans in front of their just-as-elderly querents. The fortune tellers' tables were nothing more than cardboard boxes with permanent marker lines, hardly the decorated *kumalak* rugs available to those with money. A friend said it was just a game for old women, but we could see the sincerity in their faces. The fortune teller touched each bean, her wrinkled hands feeling for spiritual signs to guide her bean sifting. The women spoke in Kazakh, not Russian, as though even their tongues would guide them to their roots. Perhaps for us, unbelievers in foreign superstitions, it would have only been a game, but if we had spoken this language, we said to ourselves, we would have sat with them, let them press the beans to our foreheads, too, and learned what the spirits of the departed wanted to tell us.

AS WE WALK UNDER THE GREEN CANOPY, we also discuss the Kazakh hospital room: yellow walls and blue light, everything dim, almost midnight and you've been in the operating room for hours. They won't let me come down to see you and I cannot communicate well enough to ask for details, they refuse to give me details, and you wake from the anesthesia fearing you are dying, crying "*муж, муж*" and then they finally wheel you to me, your skin pale and freckled like a ripe pear and, despite the nurse's warning, I hold a cup of water to your parched lips, and you choke a little, screaming from pain at the sutured incision in your abdomen.

At your admission to the hospital, a stern doctor had said, "You no have babies. No babies!" It was the only English diagnosis we'd received until the surgeon, a gentle woman with kind eyes, said "I have golden hands," the only English she spoke to us. Then, through a translator, assured us everything would be fine. She assured us the surgery had been successful, we could try for children once you were healed.

You cannot talk about the hospital or the operation without tears. Stuck as we are in this in-between, leaving Kazakhstan but not yet home, the future, pulled by conflicting prognoses, weighs heavily on us.

SOME MIGHT SAY THE SURGERY "changed our lives," but I hesitate to embrace that phrase. How can we change a life that has not yet been lived? The expression suggests that one knows what the future holds or that we might see the timelines splitting and the differences in parallel universes. To say an event *changed your life* implies that each new day, every decision, does not already change you, that you are fundamentally static unless an outside force intervenes. Maybe my love of the existential makes me curmudgeonly, perhaps privilege enables me to imagine self-actualization, but to admit that an event, a word, a realization, a squirrel, can change one's life is to admit that life is merely a sequence of shifting probabilities instead of possibilities.

But then again, perhaps the future is as much a part of us as the past: who we want to be and what we expect to be are as distinguishing features as the memories we carry with us. We cannot change the future any more than we change the past, but we can mold our expectations and re-frame our stories, which is to say, as we rearrange the images of our multiple selves, we shape our present selves.

THOUGH IT MIGHT HAVE BEEN a game for us to play at *kumalak*, it is not because we do not believe in the ability to see the future. Raised as Mormons, we believe in the gift of prophecy; we believe in a God of Revelations who will yet disclose many great and important truths. But our tradition, constrained further by a dose of secular skepticism, limits that belief to a select few seers, ignoring the gifts of those on the fringes. Still, Mormons say much about a specific, hoped-for future. As our future spanned uncertainly before us, I recalled my Patriarchal Blessing: a church leader laid his hands on my head and promised me the blessings of heaven in words specific for me. I was just fourteen, but I treasured these individual promises: a keen mind, an understanding of the will of God, fatherhood sometime "yet in the future." I trusted these blessings, let myself be guided by them, perhaps foremost because I wanted them to be true.

YOU WERE IN YOUR HOSPITAL ROOM, awaiting surgery, and your hospital roommate, two months pregnant, through broken English, said that tomorrow she would learn if "Yes baby or no baby." In the morning, she came back from the operating room, the "no baby" had been removed. It was an ill omen and it feels like yesterday still, but also a lifetime past, a past that presses on the life yet unlived.

THESE TREES CAN TELL US NOTHING, but we continue to watch them. They are quieter and more foreboding than the *kumalak* beans. These trees might as well be tarot cards with their esoteric illustrations, or horoscopes, or blessings spoken with the laying on of hands. Like essays or abstract art, fortune cookies and palm readings tell us the future only insomuch as they ask us to consider who we are, who we have been, and who we want to be, forcing us to consider the juxtapositions of so many shapes and shadows, behind which might be the thing we've always wanted.

AS I LOOK UP TO CHECK FOR SIGNS of squirrels passing overhead, I recognize that I'd never known what would happen, but I had hoped for certain outcomes. The knowledge that nothing is sure is what we are aware of now as we cross a pedestrian bridge, a commuter train passing underneath, the forest framing the cloudy sky overhead, and us together in this quiet moment waiting for tomorrow's flight home. You admire the beauty of the trees and take my hand. The tall trunks of these trees remind me of another forest walk when you were on my mind, and I recall it out loud for you:

I was walking 'round an English lake looking for red squirrels but seeing instead bluebells blooming ankle-high and the late sun barely breaking through high mists. I was thinking of you and whether or not my future had you in it. I wanted you to see the scene, too, because a narrow path lined with purple flowers and wild garlic wound its way through an emerald hillside, a near-perfect illustration of the Romantic Sublime, a moment, I knew even then, that wouldn't be perfected by squirrels, but by your seeing it with me, the same way we are now seeing these German trees, our eyes open and aching for any oracular detail, but the answers right here where our hands clasp together.

SPEAK ENGLISH, PLEASE

The twelfth-grade English lesson covered professional vocabulary and a review of suffixes, though only the girls in the front were paying any attention, the only ones able to make *ambition* into *ambitious*. The boys in the back yelled *passion* into *passionate*, but that was the example in the textbook; they were silent until *fiction* became *fictional*. Even the girls in the front row didn't know what *affection* meant, continually giving me the word *affective*, or making up things like *affectal* or *affectious*, a word I later found in the dictionary, an archaic form of *affectionate*, the word I was hoping for, so I suppose I should have given them some credit. No surprise, though, that these twelfth graders didn't know *affection*: we didn't see a lot of it here in Kazakhstan. I did see students holding hands and cuddling—even the boys were touchy with each other in a way American high school boys are not, but that is the extent of the affection. *Empathy*, too, was a new word for my twelfth and seventh graders alike. If it is here, it gets lost in the cultural differences.

On paper, this was a top school in the country, which is why officials had brought us foreigners here, to make these students the best. To make their school appear to be the best. Every child had ambition, even if it was only borrowed from their parents, many of whom were rich socialites and politicians. Mostly, the girls showed actual determination. Or rather, the boys were ambitious because their fathers said they must be, and the girls were because they could be, a difference all too obvious in the classroom.

KAZAKHSTAN, A FORMER SOVIET COUNTRY, seemed to bear the weight of its history all the way down through the educational bureaucracy. The teachers yelled at the students, shaming them into behaving well. The students complained to the administration, blaming them for the teachers' mistakes. The students, teachers, and adminis-trators all feared the politically connected parents, who funded the industry and doled out jobs. Teachers curled before them, changing the marks when asked, an easy decision because the administration punished the teachers for low grades.

WHILE COMPLETING A READING TASK, the seventh graders asked my co-teacher, Arnagul,[1] "What does *damage* mean?"

Arnagul was my partner for my three seventh-grade classes. I also worked with Sholpan for a single ninth-grade class, but for the twelfth graders, I worked alone. Team teaching was the biggest surprise of our assignments. Kirsten and I thought we had been hired for teacher development, but really, it was to be white faces in the classroom. I got lucky with my assignments: Arnagul was cheerful, resourceful, engaged with the students, constantly tried to improve her own teaching, and was a far more experienced teacher than I. A sturdy, middle-aged woman with smile wrinkles around iron-black eyes, Arnagul gave

---

[1] The names of all teachers and students in this essay have been changed.

them a quizzical look at the unknown word, then glanced at me for help.

"Antonym of *mend*?" another student asked Arnagul.

"Yep, awesome," I said. "You got it." I was surprised Arnagul didn't know that word. Her English vocabulary was better than most of the staff at the school, though perhaps not the best of all the English teachers. But a word with clear meaning for native speakers can still mean nothing to those learning the language. You only know what your textbooks tell you to know.

"Synonyms would be *break* or *hurt*," Arnagul said, still looking at me to make sure she was right. I nodded, and then another girl, Danelya, asked what *weak* meant.

"*Week*?" Arnagul asked. "W-e-e-k?"

"No, with an *a*," Danelya responded.

"Ah. Opposite of *strong*," Arnagul said, pointing to one of the boys and then flexing. "Like, Bisunkar is *strong*, and maybe, girls are *weak*."

"Oh," Danelya said, returning to her work.

Bisunkar was a skinny, wide-eyed boy with messy hair, socially awkward and un-athletic, both things Kazakh boys are meant not to be. His English was so new he wouldn't look in my direction. Danelya, on the other hand, stopped to chat whenever she saw me in the hall, detaining me to discuss the minute details of her favorite anime cartoons. Danelya, as determined a student as I have ever had, questioned everything except the answers she was given.

This is strength: The prevailing idea that boys must be made strong.

This is weakness: I did not correct her.

"SPEAK ENGLISH, PLEASE," I said to two boys who were supposed to be talking about Stonehenge, but who had devolved into Russian. Maybe they were still talking about it; I didn't have any way of knowing, but the grammar of speculation, not Stonehenge, was the real issue here.

"If I talk English, he won't understand me," one of the boys replied.

I told them to just try.

One of the great difficulties in teaching language is that you ask the students to discuss a topic, and they are happy to do so. But they want to convey meaning more than they want to practice speculative adverbs, a challenge compounded because we had no differentiated classrooms. The beginners and the experienced were all together. Everyone likes being understood, but many didn't understand my instructions. Misunderstanding teachers is upsetting for any student, but was even more frustrating, I assumed, in a culture that tolerates no error.

THE GAME WAS SIMPLE: two students would sit with their backs to the whiteboard, where I would write vocabulary; their teammates would give them definitions and panto-mimes to help them guess what I'd written.

The word: *reveal*.

I heard Ramazan, a ninth-grade boy with braces, a quick smile, and an athletic frame, shout out "Reveal!" I gave his team the point. But then my team teacher, Sholpan, yelled, "No!"

Sholpan was a thick Soviet Matron, a descendant of the Kazakh warrior women who once ruled the Steppe. She was proud of that heritage and stepped assertively through the halls, her short legs supported on tall heels.

She and I never fought, but she had frequent altercations with her other foreign team teachers. The vice principal once asked me how I got along with "that type of person."

"You did not use correct definition!" she all but screamed at Ramazan's team. "You guessed correct word, but not with right definition. It is not 'to show'; it is 'to know secret.'"

"No, it's to say a secret, to tell it, or to show something," I said.

"No, it's . . ." she trailed off. The students were looking back and forth from her to me.

I hated these moments, when her inexperience with the language shone through and the students stared with morbid curiosity. They waited silently, not sure how to react. They respected me because of my language and gender, but they also knew that students are not to question teachers; this was her classroom, and she would punish insolence. They didn't know which was more significant in this case. Often, I wanted to ask her to take a seat, pick up a pencil, and follow along as I continued. I never had those moments with Arnagul, who asked the questions she didn't understand during our planning meetings, studied the words carefully beforehand. Sholpan and Arnagul were both more experienced teachers than I and neither had asked to work with the foreigners. To her credit, I learned more from Arnagal than I offered. Sholpan only withdrew, threatened, I think, because I was male and non-confrontational. With her other international team teacher, a feisty British woman, she defended herself. With me, she only slinked away.

But these moments revealed me, too: I was pompous and arrogant because I spoke fluently. I knew there was no reason to be proud of speaking one's own tongue; it's not as though I chose English or my sex; nor have I worked particularly hard to learn words like *reveal, outrageous, damage,* or *ice rink.* They were determined for me. And yet, the advantage was mine, and I knew it. I'd been placed on a pedestal and I did little to step off from it.

One of the students saw the conceit in my eyes, and I noticed his recognition as I gave the team their point back. But he saw that arrogance as power instead, and I knew I'd not taught the lesson he actually needed.

WHEN WE FIRST ARRIVED, Kirsten and I took Russian lessons after hours from one of the local teachers, a stern-looking man who had once been part of the Red Army. He had taught Russian for decades in several countries, had learned seven or eight languages in his travels through Africa, Eastern Asia, and the Middle East, but he spoke no English. We stopped taking lessons when it became clear that we were not permitted errors. If our answer was incorrect, or if we took too long giving it, he would shout the answer in military style and move on to the next question. At first, I thought it was because he was being efficient with our time—what better way to learn the language than to go through all the tenses in one evening? But then, I felt my students' fear of inaccuracy. They wielded erasers with a frenzy. The white-out pen prevented the sword. When I let them use scratch papers on exams, their eyes filled with panic when I collected the extra sheets, no matter how much I assured them their practices would not affect their marks. They were most comfortable when I did not let them fail.

IN A LESSON ABOUT SUCCESSFUL PEOPLE, I asked the twelfth graders if they thought hard work was essential for success.

"Maybe, no," one said, not meaning "Maybe, well, no, I don't think so," but rather, "I have no strong opinion on this, but no," or maybe, "I don't want to seem like I know too much because that would make me seem different than all of you (though I am smart, but it would be rude to show it), but I think not."

"I think is luck and talent which you are born with," the same boy said.

"So, you think luck and natural ability are the most important things for success?"

"Yes, what you are born with."

"Natural talent . . ."

"Right, what you are born with and luck."

I wanted so badly to do more than correct their vocabulary and grammar, but also their worldview. But I didn't. Maybe for them, their natural talents *would* be enough, and wouldn't that be something? Maybe they will get lucky. Such a world should exist; hopefully it does somewhere, out in the stars, where the dreamt dream is ample provision for achievement.

Or maybe, they'll use what they were born with: prosperous, powerful parents. And shouldn't we all be so lucky?

I WAS OFTEN A BAD LANGUAGE teacher because of my overactive imagination. I was too willing to go with the meaning implied by the words rather than correct the grammar. For example, I saw Kirsten tutoring one of her eleventh graders about his research paper; its title read "How to Solve Problems with Stray Animals." Of course, the student meant the title to be "How to Solve the Stray Animal Problem," but his actual title is a paper I would be much more interested to read.

I suppose all sorts of problems could be solved with stray animals. Maybe we could tie inspirational quotes to the scaled feet of the small birds who were perpetually flitting about the school atrium and let those messages fall where they would. How majestic and strange the difference "Lend yourself to others, but give yourself only to yourself" would have sounded when a carrier bird landed on a Kazakh schoolboy's mind as he memorized the imperative mood; or to a teacher whose back ached constantly, who knew her students hadn't mastered the material but rounded up their grades anyhow so she wouldn't lose the money for treatments; or to the dog in the school yard who never got on the whole "stray animals are helpful" oxcart with the rest of the dummies and now lies dying in the snow, circled by ravens.

ONLY TWO OF THE TWELFTH GRADERS showed up for the lesson on leadership styles. Since I had no team teacher for the twelfth graders and there was no attendance kept, I had never been sure about whom I was supposed to contact when students didn't arrive. Most likely, they'd all been pulled away to some project I wasn't informed of, so I just continued the lesson as usual, comparing "transformational leadership," which is traditionally associated with female leaders, to "top-down," or masculine, leadership. After reading texts in favor of each style, I talked with the two students, who happened to be boyfriend and girlfriend. Both agreed that transformational leadership sounded better for employees. Both said that if they were bosses, they would be the transformational kind.

"Why is that?" I asked, and the girl responded.

"If you are nice to the people under you, they will not get you in trouble when you make a mistake," she said, succinctly summing up the Kazakh managerial style.

I asked, "If transformational leadership is more effective and women are better at that style, then why are there so few women in leadership positions in your country?" I could have asked that about *my* country, too, but high-schoolers can only think so far out. I was still trying to adjust their perspectives, and I thought staying close to home would be more effective.

They struggled quietly for a while, until the boy started to talk first.

"Well, you know," he said, looking at me, trying to invoke a male-to-male understanding, as though we shared some secret knowledge by virtue of our gender. He gestured, moving one hand higher than the other, the word *better* clearly in his eyes and at the gates of his lips. He glanced at his girlfriend and reconsidered his words. "Anciently, it has always been done," he said, a mostly factual statement if not the one that carried the full weight of his meaning. I wanted to say something about what little Kazakh history I knew, about the strong women of the clans who wielded sword and bow as deftly as the men. But I kept quiet and was rewarded by a moment every teacher longs for, a rebuttal breaking through a cultural cloud, the discomfort of disagreement obvious as the girl replied:

"But how can we change the world if we just do what has always been done?"

I FREQUENTLY TUTORED A YOUNG teacher named Damir. We were both applying for graduate schools, he in Britain and I back in the States. I helped him with his speaking and writing skills, as he needed to get his scores up for the applications. When I told him I had been accepted to Texas Tech, he said:

"Жумаисын ба! [Zhumaisin ba!]" Emphatically shaking my hand. "It means, 'Share your happiness with us!'"

I thought the phrase rather charming, and then, thinking it over, I wondered how our English *congratulations* would translate. Pondering my rudimentary knowledge of Latin roots, and then confirming my suspicions in an etymology, I found that *congratulations* means about the same thing as the Kazakh Жумаисын ба. The *con* meaning "with," and *grat* meaning that which is "agreeable," even "joyful," the whole phrase an embracing, a pulling in together, a hint of a time when communities were tighter bound.

Now, we English-speakers just mean "Good job," even when sincere, but the Kazakhs still keep the original meaning with its social implications. So little happiness lies about, what with the unwelcoming winters and the wintry working conditions—not so much physical as emotional, given the administration always looming, requesting reports and reports on reports, and redundant signatures, stamped protocols, and cutting pay when the product doesn't match the paper-trail fantasy version—I suppose they could all use more happiness, and it is only natural that when someone finds it, especially in large quantities, that it should be shared, thrown out to the celebratory crowd the way a Kazakh grandmother throws the tinsel-wrapped candies at every party.

ARNAGUL TOLD ME THAT SHE doesn't believe in superstitions, but she still pointed them out to me, obviously uncomfortable with the way I unknowingly broke Kazakh social taboos. She told me whistling inside would make me poor—one student even told me that everyone around the whistler is also made poor. I stopped whistling in the classroom and only rarely found myself whistling in the halls, but sometimes I still couldn't help it, especially as spring approached, a stark contrast from the arctic weather Kirsten and I endured for most of our time there.

My students also told me that making a *tsk* sound was bad, though no one could tell me why, except that when one boy did it, all the girls squirmed and said their grandmothers said it was bad.

But, Arnagul assured me, she did not believe in superstition. She didn't know if she believed in God. Her grandfather's tradition said she should, but she was raised Soviet. She didn't believe, but she didn't *not* believe, either. Still, whenever I put my bag on the floor next to the desk, I always found it on a chair by the end of the lesson.

"Our people have superstition," she said when I asked about it. "You mustn't put your bag on the floor."

I said, "But you don't believe in superstitions." She only responded by pursing her lips and shaking her head.

"MAYBE YOU WANT TO BE an actress or a movie star. The first problem: you are ugly."

So began the ninth graders' debate on the pros and cons of plastic surgery, a subject I wouldn't have touched, but which the English language textbook covered for a whole chapter.

"Nowadays everyone must be beautiful, so plastic surgery good if you born ugly," continued another from the pro team, and the comments commenced in similar patterns. None of them mentioned the examples they'd read in the book about people disfigured in accidents having reconstructive surgery, or even about people born with small abnormalities having minor surgeries to improve physical charisma. The whole focus was on the importance of beauty.

Then came the con side advocates, once again ignoring the information in the books, statistics about the risks of the procedures.

"It is our inner beauty that matters," a boy said.

"God made us all different," another boy said. "Not like mosquitoes."

"Ay, yes!" Sholpan said, standing and rising almost to the boy's height. She smiled at him, encouraging him. "God! Yes. See, this is critical thinking."

The boy continued, "We each have our own dried grape."

I asked him what that meant, but he couldn't explain. The other students tried to help, the whole class suddenly exploding into conversation. Eventually, I gathered that the Russian word изюминка (*iz-yoo-MEEN-ka*), which can only be translated as "raisinness," is the essential word in a common idiom: "Everyone has their own raisinness." Everyone has one thing, however small and wrinkled, that sweetens the cake.

LATE IN THE SEMESTER, most of the international teachers and many of the local teachers were required to attend a meeting about proctoring a national math exam. At the front of the classroom, a Kazakh language teacher spoke while an English teacher translated. They explained how long each exam would be, how to start the exam, how to fill in the bubble sheets, what the students would be allowed to have with them during the exam. They explained how the students should fill in the personal information at the top. Someone asked if the students would be allowed to have another answer sheet if they messed up.

"Students are not permitted to make mistakes," the translator said before the presenter even responded.

Kirsten and I looked askance at each other and chortled to ourselves. The translator didn't mean exactly what she said, but of course it was accurate nonetheless.

ONCE, I ENCOUNTERED DAMIR as he was leaving the teacher workroom and I was about to go in. Shaking hands is an important custom for men in Kazakhstan, so I immediately offered my hand, but Damir pulled back.

"Either before or after," he said, though I didn't know what he meant until he pointed down at the line on the floor, the space between the hallway's carpet and the workroom's tile. "Either before or after," he repeated, and then he shook my hand when I entered the room entirely. Damir, like Arnagul, has also expressed to me his atheistic belief, but this was not the first time he insisted on observing old superstitions. He also stopped me from congratulating him on the birth of his daughter because it was not safe to do so until after forty days. Good news is often short-lived.

He did not stop me from congratulating him when he told me he had been accepted into an excellent British graduate school with a government-funded, full-ride scholarship.

DURING A CLASS WITH THE seventh graders, I was running through the basic academic essay structure. This late in the year, they knew their introductions and were doing excellently on their thesis statements. Most of them were consistently producing simple topic sentences, but Arnagul and I were just introducing conclusion paragraphs when I asked, "What does *summarize* mean?"

The room was silent. No one knew, so no one offered an answer because to offer an incorrect one, especially in a room full of peers eager to point out flaws, would be insufferable. Better silence. Finally, one boy bravely raised his chubby hand and, his voice full of uncertainty, said, "A Japanese warrior?"

ANOTHER LESSON, STILL IN THE chapter about plastic surgery:

"What about our religion?" Sholpan asked, standing squarely and honorably at the front of the classroom as she asked a question that, had we been in America, would have gotten her or both of us fired. "The Kazakh religion is Muslims. We do not allow plastic surgery."

I was silent. I hadn't been trained how to deal with teachers asserting their religious views on students. I knew how to keep students on topic, but had little skill in keeping a fellow teacher there. But I didn't need to. The ninth graders, noticing Sholpan's slowly eroding ethos, defended themselves.

"I knew a woman, she is Muslim," a girl says, gesturing around her neck and head to imply a hijab, "and she got plastic surgery."

"Well, it is not allowed. This is a Muslim country."

Another student mumbled out an ever-present Kazakh *maybe*: "Maybe some people think this is the 21st Century and Muslim isn't real."

I didn't know where his defiance came from. It was not a popular opinion, even among the students, but Sholpan had lost so much respect with the class that the students now felt comfortable speaking blasphemies in front of her. I knew by the way they looked at me that my presence had something to do with the change. I hoped it was because of my patience with them, or maybe my willingness to explain answers, but I doubted it.

IN THE SAME MEETING ABOUT the standardized math exam, we were told that the students could not use pens.

Someone asked, "What if a student forgets a pencil?"

"Such problems never occur," the translator responded, as though she'd never, not even once, anywhere in the world, stood in front of high school students.

I was the one who asked the real doozy of a question, the hot topic that most of the local teachers wanted us to avoid: "How should we proceed when we find someone cheating?"

The classroom erupted immediately into chaos, mostly in Kazakh and Russian. I didn't think most of the teachers spoke English, but they must have learned the word *cheating* from us: we'd said it enough times in the previous weeks.

"Don't allow them to cheat," the translator at the front responded. "There should be enough of you that they will not be able to."

Of course we teachers were powerless to prevent it. On the very exam in question, two of my students did cheat while I watched helplessly. One student wrote the answer on the corner of her test booklet and then slowly moved the paper so that her friend could see the answer. Had this happened in America, I would have taken both papers immediately. Here, I was only permitted to give a warning. I could have told my department head, but she had no power to do anything else, for fear of parents who came down like wrathful vultures. We foreign teachers didn't have contracts that the parents could touch so we were never given power to enforce rules. Instead, I only whispered to the girls to keep their eyes on their own papers, and for the rest of the exam, I stood over them, glaring, making sure they saw me looking every time they glanced up.

DURING A SEMI-WEEKLY principal's meeting with all the teachers, we were berated by the vice principals. We were told exactly how many students had a Two (equivalent to a D, though essentially an F since we are not permitted to give Ones or Zeros). Threes are technically "Good," but still shameful. Each department's counts were read aloud.

We the international staff knew these Twos—and most of the Threes—were our fault. We were the ones who insisted on criteria-based marking, on the use of rubrics. No one mentioned that these new techniques were standardizing the results. They only saw the sea of Fives and Fours drying up as a bell-curve developed.

One of the vice principals yelled in Kazakh for ten minutes, the whole room quiet as her face turned red and spittle flew from her lips. We leaned over to ask a colleague for a translation, but were told that none was needed. The woman eventually did pause and look toward the assigned translator, who had been quivering in the back, holding the microphone like it would protect her. The entire ten-minute tirade was translated only as this: "If the students are getting bad marks, it is your fault. It is your teaching. It is your work to do their best and pass their exams."

In these moments, it was better to think that something was lost in translation, to wish that what I understood the words to mean could be blamed on the less-than-perfect English that I was here to help correct.

AS THE TERM CAME TO AN END, one of the twelfth graders came up to me before class started.

"I got into a university!" she said enthusiastically, though not with as much excitement as I would have expected. I'd tutored her on the entrance essays, and I knew how excited she was about college, and how much she—so much more than many of her peers—deserved a good education.

"Which one?" I asked, assuming it was the local university our school was designed to feed into.

"The University of Maine," she said, "and Westminster College, in Utah."

"Excellent!" I said, telling her how much I had loved living in Utah.

"But I only got a half scholarship," she replied. "They only gave out ten full scholarships."

I assured her that if they gave out that few of them, then getting a half scholarship was still really good.

"Yeah," she replied, "but I won't be able to afford it on just a half scholarship. I'll probably go to a school in Moscow or stay here."

I suggested she look for other scholarships, especially from the many big companies and organizations that helped foreign students go to American universities.

She nodded, keeping her eyes down.

"I cannot get such scholarships," she said, "because I do not have any relatives in big companies." She turned away, ending the conversation, and returned to her seat as class started.

It was in those conversations I was reminded that not all of my students were the children of the elite. Some of them had earned their way into this prestigious school. Some of them deserved more than we were giving. They had worked hard but didn't have the same luck.

"I TRANSLATED A RUSSIAN PROVERB FOR YOU," Damir told me as I sat to join him in the faculty cafeteria. "A man goes to café. Waiter tells the man, 'Would you like coffee or tea?' and the man says, 'Coffee.' 'No,' The waiter says, 'You did not guess. Tea.'" He laughed.

But, like warm weather, these laughs were fleeting. Which is to say, he didn't give details and I didn't ask for them when he announced that our school's administration successfully conspired to prevent his leaving and had his scholarship to Britain revoked. I mourned for him and gave my condolences as I recognized once again the freedoms I enjoyed. I had chosen to be here, and so I was free to leave.

AFTER ARNAGUL AND I FINISHED our classes' end-of-term speaking exams, we looked over the scores together, making sure we had correctly recorded everything. It was a difficult exam, so there were some Twos and only a few Fives.

Arnagul pointed to one boy's score and gave a small grunt of disapproval. "Sultan deserves to get a Five because he tried so hard," Arnagul said.

"Yes, but he only earned a Four. His vocab and grammar just weren't what they should have been."

"It is a shame," she said, and I was sure she would change the grade when I wasn't looking.

I was no longer surprised by her disregard for the grades. When we first started working together, she told me it was a shame that Dias—one of our weaker students—always got such low marks, "because he has such nice parents." It doesn't help, either, that this was Dias's first year of English instruction and that several of his classmates had lived in the United States and others had English teachers for parents. The lack of differentiation ruined his chances of passing the assignments, but somehow, he had always been rounded up to a Three. Now, I saw that her fixed grades were not motivated by compassion for him. I now knew that too many Twos would shrink her already meager paycheck. Unable to condone her stance or the administration's harsh retributions, I remained silent.

"Should we give Sanzhar more points? Dias scored the same as him," Arnagul said, looking at the bottom of the list.

Sanzhar was funnier than Dias, more popular with the other students, and it would have been embarrassing for him to be seen as equal to Dias. But Dias had been studying and had actually earned his Three this time, though Arnagul didn't appear to see that. On this point, I didn't budge. A Three was passing. Sanzhar had also earned his

Three. Besides, I knew that Arnagul would later change the grades as she wished when she entered them into the school records, which the international teachers weren't allowed to see or touch.

WITH THE EXAMS OVER, I divided up the papers with my team teachers. Arnagul and Sholpan both left the essay portion of the exams for me to grade, taking the multiple-choice portions for themselves. Even though I half-seriously complained to Kirsten, I didn't mind. The five-paragraph essay has been in my DNA since middle school and I knew that neither of my co-teachers felt comfortable with thesis statements or topic sentences. Divvying out the essays to me was a way to avoid the task without admitting weakness. Except, Arnagul *did* admit her weakness, in a way: after I graded the essays, she asked me questions about why one paper was better than the other, how I determined the scores. She took notes when asking about the difference between an expository and a persuasive essay. Sholpan, worried about the deadline for submitting grades, only asked me if I had finished yet. I didn't blame either of them for giving me the lion's share of grading. We international teachers often judged our local peers for their early hours and late nights, but we were too harsh. Our colleagues did what they needed to survive. They frequently trudged through the day with migraines, going to message specialists in the dark hours after school. They understood the system more than I did; they saw its flaws better than I did. Being insiders, they weren't in a position to complain. As outsides, we had no power to change anything.

On any given day, Sholpan and Arnagul were both at school well before I arrived and often stayed far later. I didn't ask about wages, but I assumed I made more than twice what they did, plus the perks of holidays and housing they did not receive. They wrote more reports, did more tutoring, organized special projects, and understood our bosses' ten-minute tirades that, for me, were softened through translation.

Administrators told us not to return graded exams back to students, only to report their marks. But, they said, we were still required to comment on the exams anyhow in case parents were upset with their children's marks. I was told by the English department head that I must write in pencil in case they needed to change a mark or comment, but I wrote with ink, pretending ignorance, a small defiance.

For the most part, I was pleased with my students' work. The essays were formulaic, to be sure, stereotypical explanations of what they will do on their summer holidays, but I was thrilled that they'd mastered the formula. The theses were perfectly placed, the topic sentences crisp, if bland.

And then, at the end of one of the last essays I graded, I noticed a comment that reminded me where I worked. The marginalia from the same student who had introduced me to *raisinness*, now seeing my grading for what it was: "Thanks for wasting your golden time checking my essay."

Finally, someone, anyone, willing to speak up, even in the margins.

"You're welcome," I wrote, though he'll never see it.

IF WE HAD BEEN
ALLOWED TO TAKE PICTURES

O utside of Almaty's Cathedral of the Holy Ascension, we took pictures of the park grounds, the painted spires, and the many white-tailed squirrels that occupied the trees. If we had been allowed to take pictures inside the Cathedral of the Holy Ascension, this is the picture I would have taken:

A woman cleans the wax from the base of the candelabras. She wears a brown and orange dress, simple, made of sturdy material, like a pillowcase or a craft project, and over that, a blue apron. Like the other workers and all the female worshipers, she has covered her head. She wears a blue kerchief, the same thick material as the apron, tying back her hair, accentuating the creases in her copper face with its wide, beautiful expanse of Kazakh cheeks. Her narrow eyes look only at her task. She has a paintbrush in one hand, and with it she sweeps the dripped, dry remains of prayers off the bronze candelabra into her left hand, cupped at the cusp.

Behind her, the Virgin watches from a tapestry, the woodwork of the cathedral worked in gold, a home for a king, the King, and his Virgin Mother. Behind the images, a single ray of sunlight penetrates a rose and aqua window above. It illuminates the icons, gives added glimmer to the gold-flecked craftsmanship, and creates a single blotch of light on the floor, but mostly the ray highlights the dimness of this place, its sacred dark. Old women stoop to the ground, crossing themselves over and over again as they approach the altar with muttered prayers, shuffling toward that light.

However, this woman does not work in the ray of light, but rather beneath it, still in the recessive shadows where the blue of her apron and the orange of her dress are both just brown-gray, and the icons watch her from the lit dome above, their eyes untroubled and glittering. She is not in darkness, though. No, here is the candlelight, gold on her face, warm on her aged skin, flickering in her black eyes, separating her from the others, mere worshipers who step close to light the candle, only to step away and look at the Virgin stitched in the tapestry or the Christ nailed on the wall or at the shoes muddy on their feet. But she has no fear of this fire; she looks capably into the radiant heat of these prayers, her brush working devotedly between burning beeswax. Her fingers do not flinch from the flame even as she pinches out the last petal of an almost spent taper, plucks it from the holder, and adds it to the weight of melted hopes in her capable hand.

~~MY~~ OUR LIBRARY

If you arrange your books according to their contents you are
sure to get an untidy shelf. If you arrange your books accord-
ing to their size and colour you get an effective wall.

—A. A. Milne "My Library"

L ike Milne, we've moved into a new house this morning. Kirsten and I signed the mortgage papers, picked
up the keys, drove to the animal rescue to adopt a kitten,
and then came to our new home, our first house. For a few
minutes, we sat on the carpet watching the kitten explore
the empty living room, the Texas light streaming in from
a large window. Then new friends and strangers spent the
afternoon helping us unload the moving truck, and now
I sit in the room that will be my office and library—a
whole room!— The shelves are haphazardly full of quickly
unpacked books and so, like Milne's books, mine are not
where they should be, but instead, where they are. In the
past, my books, if they were organized at all, were arranged
by topic. But I'm thinking about organizing by color this
time, an idea I got from seeing several friends who did
the same—I see now that the idea may have come from
Milne, though I only returned to his essay after the fact.

As Kirsten unpacked something somewhere else in the
house, I stood in my library and considered how to tackle

the project. There are logistical difficulties because our shelves are not all the same height or shape, so a book's size will be a factor. What few books have already been unpacked have mostly been placed by size so as not to destabilize the shelves, thus my Penguin Press editions of four-inch tall essays by Montaigne (godfatherly red), Bacon (noble blue), and Hazlitt (slightly angrier red) are rather rudely stacked next to other minuscule bindings regardless of color, which I don't think Montaigne would mind, but Hazlitt, only four-inches tall as I have him, would rather Bacon be on another shelf. But then, Hazlitt would prefer to lay all the books on other shelves. Bacon, logical as always, would prefer Montaigne be on the shelf with other books containing Montaigne, perhaps with Sarah Bakewell's stark-white biography, *How to Live*, which, because it is tall, is currently on the bottom shelf where I've placed the heavier books for counterbalance. Heavy as it is, Bakewell's hardback is likely to be sandwiched between courser, more pedestrian texts that are similar only in size and weight, perhaps the bland-white *Handwriting Analysis: Putting It to Work for You* and the dramatic black with cab-yellow lettering *Comics Crash Course*, leftovers from past enthusiasms that never quite stuck but which I will not part with.

Now that I say it, I'm curious what books Bakewell's biography of Montaigne is actually sandwiched between, and I have to get up to check. The results are not as base as I had thought: to the left sits Silverstein's jacketless *Where the Sidewalk Ends*, rather worn and dusty from a childhood of reading, and to the right hunkers the grand-paternal, silver-gray and creased *Diagnostic and Statistical Manual for Mental Disorders*, 4th edition, a remnant from Kirsten's graduate work in counseling. (You see, I have titled this essay "My Library," after Milne, but really it should be "Our Library." Perhaps I say "my" because I am egotistical; this may be true, but it may also be because I have a greater investment in the books as an English graduate student, or perhaps only because the shelves are close to my desk, whereas Kirsten's desk will eventually be in our bedroom, but even there we have complications because my desk—heavy and solid, a faux-finish in forest green—is a piece of furniture Kirsten brought to our marriage, though as a workspace it has been almost entirely mine. And while we're on the subject of mingling, I should say that the color-coordinating project may have been Kirsten's suggestion first and she is as excited as I am to undertake it but also restrained enough to be looking for our dishes rather than rummaging through partially unpacked books.) Other books close at hand to *How To Live* include *Intermediate Tagalog* in glossy white; *Tales of a Triumphal People: A History of Salt Lake Country, UT,* a sort of tepid orange; Madden's *Quotidiana*, chalkboard black; Spandel's *The 9 Rights of Every Writer: A Guide For Teachers*, maroonish, but so many different colors in the lettering so as to be distracting; and Glück's *The Wild Iris* in gold and black with traces of a green so similar to the desk's hue that I've pulled it out to admire the shades together. When Kirsten and I eventually get to organizing these by color, *Wild Iris* will likely end up near Fadiman's *Ex Libris*, a pale green. The current proximities will not last. At the moment, though, Fadiman is accompanied by a sky-blue W.S. Merwin, French-gray Ron Carlson, and a black, self-published science fiction novel by my uncle.

I've yet to read any of these three books, but a collector's hope springs eternal.

Curious about proximities, I just rechecked the shelf where we'd put the diminutive books, my favorite of which are two miniature hymn books bound in fraying cloth; we acquired them from an estate sale simply for their pleasing cardinal color. Montaigne and Bacon were there with the short books, just where I thought they would be, but Hazlitt had gone a-journeying, and it was some time before I found him again in a stack of books and papers on my desk. On top of the stack were blank greeting cards with their envelopes, then the office-paper white *Nikon D90 User's Manual*, Charles Doss's olive green *I Shall Mingle: Poems and Essays*, then Hazlitt turned aside so I couldn't see his spine, all atop two parti-colored children's workbooks: *United States Geography* and the *Rand McNally Kids' Road Atlas* (Kirsten is ready to pass her love of maps on to our yet-to-be-conceived children).

That it took me some time to realize there was a stack of books on my desk at all tells you something about the state of my desk: all the drawers and cabinets still empty, their someday contents spilled across its top and at its feet, where the kitten sleeps in an emptied box. There are empty CD jewel cases, business envelopes, a journal, the Bluetooth keyboard for Kirsten's iPad, a picture of my mother, scissors, old travel maps from cities we've never been to, a notebook, utility bills. In fact, the only thing on the desk right now that will actually belong on rather than in the desk when I finally get around to organizing it are the computer I am currently typing at, one of two desk lamps, and the lion's skull. The pile of books will remain, ever-shifting like a sand dune.

I did do some arranging when I unpacked the first few office boxes, but, ever eager, I focused almost entirely on the books, already beginning to place them by color, since, as Milne says, we must not be shy to admit that our books are ornamentation. Yes, we readers and literary types mean to read them when we purchase them, but that doesn't always happen. Instead, we place them where we might look at them and then buy more before we even get around to reading the ones we've already purchased. There is a sentimental acquisition of books, buying what we like to think of ourselves reading, not what we actually have time to read (though we read plenty.) The collection grows faster than we can keep up.

When I started organizing by color, the thought of having memoirs scattered throughout the science fiction novels and the poetry mingled profanely amongst the religious reference works drove me a bit batty, but I had a good start at it, getting three boxes unloaded from off the floor and a single, (our shortest) bookcase thoroughly colorized: the top shelf started in white, faded into red, then merged into grays and blacks at the other end. In the middle shelf I arranged my brightly colored paperback versions of *The Best American Essay* and *The Best American Short Story* collections, using their brightly colored spines as markers rather than the collection date, making for a rainbow of a shelf that sprinkled in reprinted classics with contemporarily bright bindings such as *Gulliver's Travels, One Hundred Years of Solitude* and *Things Fall Apart*.

Then, Kirsten pointed out that with at least six library boxes still to unpack, my quaint little color scheme would fall apart quickly. She suggested there might be more pressing matters, such as getting the dishes unpacked and the kitchen in a state where we could do more than make peanut butter and jelly sandwiches. Perhaps, she implied, we would want to sleep with sheets on the bed tonight, which would mean finding the box with the linens. Besides, she reminded me, she was excited about the book organizing, too, and asked that I wait to let her help. I gave our library one last glance, then returned to the kitchen to search for sauce pans.

THE LIBRARY REMAINED with its haphazard piles and premature schema for several more days, joined by even more books because as we unpacked, we found them in all sorts of boxes, even when the label read "Clothing" or "Bathroom." Whole boxes of books that hadn't been labeled at all, except as "Heavy." Piles of itinerant volumes grew, and it soon became apparent that we wouldn't have enough space on the shelves for all of our books. We'd lost a shelf in the move—cheap press board, it had died of dysentery while crossing the Rockies. Furthermore, we'd acquired more things. We were mingling together the long-term storage we'd kept in Utah, the souvenirs we'd brought back from a year in Kazakhstan, the books I'd gotten for my new graduate studies and teaching responsibilities, plus the last boxes from our parents' attics and basements which they'd recently unloaded on us, telling us we were now adult enough to store our own crap.

But even when I returned from the home furnishing store with another shelf, it remained unassembled, yet another box to be unpacked. And eager as I was, Kirsten made me promise I'd not start organizing in earnest until she was there to help. Besides, getting the couch uncovered so we could have a place seemed important. As did finding the clothes appropriate for our new jobs.

Kirsten finally set up the shelf one evening, fighting with the stuff on the floor for space to lay out the planks, while I sat at this green desk grading student work, feeling slightly guilty for doing a labor that looked like lazing around while she did the more strenuous duty, reassuring myself that she enjoyed it, puzzle enthusiast that she is. By the time we both finished our tasks, neither of us had the energy to fill the shelf, and it remained empty for several days.

One day I returned home from work to find that Kirsten had unpacked the rest of the boxes, filling the remaining shelves as was convenient to clear the floor, not as made any real sense for a library, and not at all by color, size, or even subject. For a brief moment, I thought she'd given up on the color-coding scheme, but she assured me it was temporary.

"We'll get to it soon," she said. "Don't worry."

I did worry. Would this new, definitely convenient-for-floor-space-but-less-so-for-finding-things organization make a long-term arrangement more or less trouble? Also, I was curious where books had landed. *Handwriting Analysis* is on the new shelf, not the one I'd unpacked, and shares its shelf space with a red display copy of *Pinocchio*, a black *Peyton Place*, the red box set of *Kirsten: An American Girl*, and my blue-gray undergraduate honors thesis, a science fiction novel so filled with typos I wonder how it ever got past the thesis committee. My original color-centric exploration in organization looks at once childish and jewel-toned against the organic entropy of her unpacking.

Kirsten had also gathered the knickknacks, placing them together roughly against the books and on top of the shelves. We keep no curio in the house, no shelf entirely for keepsakes, but we mingle mementos with the books. These shelves are our only showcase, mostly for ourselves. Many of the keepsakes are from our travels: a carved water buffalo from the Philippines, a leather-bound yurt from Kazakhstan, a photo of a rustic Guatemalan door, calligraphy blossoms from Beijing's Forbidden Palace. None of these were placed with any purpose other than to get them out of boxes, so they are laid across the books, jammed up against other trinkets that aren't as exotic but are still sentimental: glass bottles we decorated our wedding reception with, a blue and white Japanese tea set from her mother, the handcrafted scarecrow doll from mine, a globe with oceans of cream and countries of turquoise and gold. With the books, the trinkets will become our own display of memories and good times, the books and souvenirs equal partners in reminding us of who we are, of what we find valuable; the library will become our own personal *wunderkammer*.

ONE RAINY SUNDAY AFTERNOON—though bedroom furniture still loitered in the living room and homeless appliances occupied the kitchen—Kirsten and I began the library organization in earnest. I'd spent enough time pining over the books and excitedly talking about color-coding that Kirsten began to fear I'd take on the project solo. And though it had been fun to search for Dillard's *Pilgrim at Tinker Creek* and in the process stumble upon Marquis and Haskell's appropriately pale yellow 1964 "definitive guide to cheese," McCarthy's all-black *The*

Road, or my grandfather's *American College Dictionary*, it was time for order. Kirsten and I began by moving all the trinkets to the tops of the shelves until we were ready to intermingle them, then took the issue seriously in hand by putting Hazlitt back on a shelf where he belongs, right beside an orange-creamy Charles Lamb, who, as we all know, plays well with everyone and is, more to the point, about the same height and complexion. As we removed and replaced books, the kitten took advantage of the shifting spaces and danced among the shelves, and thus we spent the afternoon, assembling our library.

PIE MONTH

Pesto Chicken and Artichoke

Because we love pie, Kirsten and I always celebrate Pi Day: March 14 (3.14). But because 3.14 could also designate all of March 2014, and because Pie Month happens only once every hundred years, I decided we should have pie every day that month. Once Kirsten sort of agreed, I added that I didn't mean leftovers. "We can't do this half-way. Only once in a century!" I said. We stood in front of the fridge, where so many such conversations happen. "We have to have a new pie every day."

So, on the first of March, 2014, while Kirsten and I were visiting Seattle, she searched Pike Place Market for fish, as any self-respecting foodie would, and I looked for pie. She returned with sushi and I came back with a pesto chicken and artichoke pasty from a bagel stand—a fancy bagel stand, because this was Pike Place.

Key Lime and Peach-Raspberry

When God served up punishment after Adam and Eve partook of the forbidden fruit, there was a clear indication of the relationship Adam would have with the world. He would toil for food. He would till the ground till return-ing to it. By the sweat of his face, he would eat his bread. "Thorns and thistles," the Lord said. "In sorrow shalt thou eat." Of course, it's hard to think of sorrow when eating pie, though we did consider the increase in butter we would need for the experiment, a direct ding to an already thin budget and our increasing waistlines.

There was sorrow elsewhere, if you backtracked far enough. Most of our butter-buying income came from Kirsten, an eighth-grade history teacher. It was a job she'd started a few months prior, mid-school year because the previous teacher had walked out, literally, leaving her things behind. Kirsten's students were bad and proud of it. This followed the year of teaching in Kazakhstan, where Kirsten's responsibilities had reduced her to tears several times, and prior to that—our first year of marriage—she'd also hated her teaching job in Utah.

I always felt a little guilty because I loved my job, even in Kazakhstan, where we worked for the same school, and where I managed to stay low-key and low-responsibility while administrators seemed to gang up on Kirsten. But I did feel the pressure of Adam's call to work. "By divine design," states the Mormon Church's Proclamation on the Family, "fathers are to provide the necessities of life." I was not yet a father—we'd been trying since we returned from Kazakhstan, but to no avail. My job was currently just a part-time grad student gig at Texas Tech in Lubbock. Feeling I could do more, I looked elsewhere for work and started teaching online for another university, so I could provide a few more necessities. Like, say, more pie.

Sausage, Tomato, and Cheese

In Kazakhstan, we learned a Russian adage: "You never ruin the porridge with butter." This is also true of savory pies and cheese.

I thought of this as I rummaged through our kitchen the third night of Pie Month. We'd returned to Lubbock from Seattle the night before. Kirsten had the car, and I needed to leave for class when she returned. There had to be pie on the table; I had to use what was on hand. Luckily, making up recipes on the spot is my forte, an ancestral trait perhaps, as my mother had a name for it: leftover surprise. I pulled things out of the fridge and got to mixing. Cheddar, mozzarella, feta whipped with egg, poured into red ramekins with spicy sausage and sun-dried tomatoes.

When she returned home, tired and hungry, Kirsten was surprised to find I'd made a dinner that smelled so nice, perhaps because I had a lot of work to do after a weekend away. Cooking, like most arts, is best done while procrastinating. Another aphorism, this one James Richardson: "All work is the avoidance of harder work." Or perhaps Kirsten was surprised because the pies looked quite nice, the red ramekins highlighting the warm tones of the cheese and tomatoes, browned and crusty.

Kirsten said it was the best pie she'd ever had. Unfortunately, by the time Pie Month ended, Kirsten still said this was the best she'd ever had.

Apple Walnut

We'd just bought our first house, an Eden we didn't know how to tend.

Our fathers provided examples of handyman-ness, especially her father, Brad, an architect. We were always hearing about new projects, each more luxurious than the last. For example, Brad had recently built a covered deck in his backyard. It was perfect, each detail something you'd see in *Sunset* magazine, the company my father worked for most of my childhood, which meant that our house was filled with glossy images of domestic style, models of perfect homes and gardens. However, like my mother, I was more concerned with *Sunset*'s cookbooks than with the house's design or upkeep.

My father-in-law had volunteered to knock out our dining room wall to install a sliding door into the backyard. It wouldn't be trouble, he said, because he already needed to deliver the shelf he'd designed for the antique player-piano rolls Kirsten inherited from her mother.

Kirsten and I discussed her parents' upcoming trip as we shared the day's slice: store-bought, shelled in molded plastic, too small, too sweet. We were hoping for good news to share when her parents visited, to have ultrasound pictures to hang on the fridge, something more than what she normally told them over the phone: "We're still trying."

But even if she was a few weeks along in the summer, odds were Kirsten would be out helping her dad or grilling the steaks, and I'd be in the kitchen chopping greens for the Caesar salad. But as we sat in the grocery store café, sharing pie, there was no indication that her "condition" would be an issue.

Mac 'n Cheese Pie

I was taught to believe in a historical Eden. Though my father didn't doubt the story's allegorical or symbolic nature, there was no doubt in his retelling that Adam and Eve actually lived, actually fell, went from pre-mortal to mortal. The science of the issue is muddy, especially for a church that doesn't shun evolution. In introductory biology and science classes at BYU, professors distribute packets—fuzzy from generations of photocopying—of quotes from church leaders discussing and disagreeing on issues around evolutionary science, including theories of pre-Adamites. The main emphasis of the packet: you can be an evolutionist, but Adam was real, even if we don't know when, exactly, the Fall happened in the fossil record.

We cannot forget Adam and Eve because their story is the key to Mormon culture. It's their story we see in the temple ceremonies, the highest form of worship. During that presentation, we're told to "consider yourselves as if you were respectively Adam and Eve."

Their basic story—disobedience, punishment, struggle, repentance, and then redemption—is easy enough to see in myself. Were there not two characters but one, were the punishments for Adam and Eve exactly the same, were the changes of culture over time clearly shown in the telling, I would have no trouble considering myself Adam and Eve. It's the *respectively* that vexes me.

Eve takes the brunt of the rub, and as feminists who want to believe but aren't sure of the story's full significance, Kirsten and I take issue.

Cauliflower Pie with Potato Crust

If we are to believe the Lord's grammar—with so many murky years of translation—then Adam's sin was not just that he ate of the fruit, but that he did so after hearkening unto Eve. Which is to say, you can read his punishment coming because he followed the woman. Which exacerbates the story's misogyny. Adam will sweat, will work, work, die. His pain is all of the body. But for Eve, sorrow. Sorrow multiplied in labor and conception. It isn't just the different bodily punishments here, which are clearly the most mythological, but the stating of order. Adam must follow the Lord, but Eve must follow Adam. Why? We don't know, but Kirsten and I reread Genesis that month, asking ourselves why. Because Adam follows the rules when the snake tempts him, because Adam is being reminded that he is in charge, because men wrote the story?

And so her husband will rule over her. To make things worse, he will also, on occasion, feed her potato crust that tastes like dictionary pages and fill it with vegetable mash too salty to be truly desirable. The only saving grace will be the cheese, plentifully applied.

Four-Berry Ice Cream Pie

A few weeks previous, our furnace gave out on the second coldest night of winter, which was followed by the coldest night, 13°F, cold enough to freeze the kitchen pipes. We thought it was just the pilot light, an easy fix, though Kirsten looked up instructions online before we attempted it because no one wants to accidentally blow up a house—especially a new house. But the pilot wouldn't light, and we were ninety percent sure we did it right. She called her brother for advice. I called a repair company, who said they could come the following Monday. By then, we envisioned, all our pipes would have burst, and we would be bundled in arctic gear, cuddling under the covers to prevent hypothermia.

I sent an email to the men's group at church asking to borrow space heaters. A man we didn't know volunteered to take a look at the furnace and followed us home after church services. He once owned a heating and air conditioning company and kept saying, "This is fun," as he tinkered with the heater.

Ten dollars for a broken part and an hour later, the heat was back on, leaving me with the song "Come On Baby, Light My Fire," stuck in my head, which was particularly ironic and disturbing because the week the fire gave out was the same week Kirsten recommended we up our chances for conception by using an app that tracked her ovulation, telling us the optimal time for sex, a schedule so precise that I had been unable to perform all week, despite suggestions it was the best time.

And the problem lingered.

Mormon Mocha Mousse

Because Kirsten was away visiting her sister in Colorado, I took the day off from writing, grading, and reading to bake pies. I purchased vanilla wafers for crumb crusts, and eggs, cream, and chocolate for custards and mousses. I knew we would eventually have work we couldn't avoid, days with no time for messes in the kitchen, so I stocked the freezer with ready-to-go pastries. I pressed butter and crushed wafers into miniature, disposable tins. I rolled out traditional pie dough, not much more than flour, salt, and shortening. Then, in a chaos of bowls, mixed the fillings. Salted caramel banana, turkey potpies, curried apple and mushroom, mango float, apple cheddar. All would wait for Kirsten.

On the phone that night, Kirsten assured me she'd kept the pact; she'd eaten pizza for lunch. I told her about the pies, and she made me promise to save her a bite of the Mormon mocha—chocolate flavored with Pero, a roasted barley powder, instead of espresso. This is one of her favorite pies; I should have waited to serve it, but it was the one I wanted. I also wanted her to appreciate my versatility. On some level, I knew Pie Month was about showing how clever I was coming up with all these new pies, which meant I needed to save these other pies for nights when she could be suitably impressed.

I didn't feel at all clever as I spooned the mocha mousse straight from the tin, my not-thin belly resting against the faux-wood countertop, alone in the house, selfishly feeling a little betrayed that she'd go anywhere during Pie Month. Then, I wiped the cookie crumbs into my palms, washed my hands, and went to bed.

Mango Float

Kirsten was convinced my impotence was only temporary. "I never should have told you about the schedule app," she said.

Just because I'm a man doesn't mean I'm oblivious to the ovarian cycle. I know when her period is, know that the fertile window comes two weeks later. I didn't need the app to point out the calendar. Still, somehow talking about the ideal time made the whole thing seem insurmountable. Though I don't consider myself a stressed person, it seemed my to-do list for school and work, the deadlines, and this new deadline, were all just too much for the little guy. I didn't want to believe that potential fatherhood was stressful. I felt completely fine with the idea. If I had doubts, they hadn't registered. A baby was the next step in our life together.

So, more worried than I let on to Kirsten, I went to the Internet, which said that though erectile dysfunction is associated with emotional stress, it's much more commonly a physical malady. It could be diabetes, WebMD said, cautioning me to worry if I felt excessively thirsty or had to pee often, which I then did every time I had to pee or needed water. I've always been one to drink a lot of water, though. Maybe that meant I'd had diabetes a long time and never realized it? And then, when we tried to make love and I had the smallest inclination to pee first, I worried again.

Burrito Pie

Traditional Christian rhetoric paints Eve as the great sinner, the enticer, the one who lost us Paradise forever.

But as we reread Genesis during Pie Month, we had questions, mostly Kirsten who posited them to me from the couch with the Bible in her lap while I layered tortillas with beans and cheese: "How could she sin if she didn't yet know the difference between good and evil?"

She asked again while I served burrito pie on our blue and white plates, which she'd been collecting since before we were married: "The serpent, always dealing in halves and pieces, spoke the truth when he said they would become like the gods, knowing good and evil. So was Eve tricked or did she see the truth for what it was and seek to know light from darkness, pleasure from pain, transgression followed by the joy of redemption?"

As we picked at leftover mango float: "What I really don't understand is what that means for us. Eve was told to follow Adam, but 'they twain shall be one flesh.' 'Neither is the man without the woman, neither the woman without the man.' Am I supposed to follow you? Because that doesn't feel right either."

"I don't know that I want to lead, or to be the one in charge," I said as we cleaned up. "Do you feel like we're unequal?"

"No, and thank you for that."

Oatmeal Creme Pie

Kirsten texted me at lunchtime to say she'd bought an Oatmeal Creme Pie for a snack and would prefer a light dinner.

I had already bought Oatmeal Creme Pies, knowing they're Kirsten's favorite junk-snack and knowing they would be fun on a day we didn't have time to cook. I'd hidden them on the top shelf of the pantry, behind the herbal teas, too high for Kirsten to see.

I took down the little packages and ate mine alone, standing at the counter, having never considered before that one could be miserable while eating childhood treats.

How now to spend the afternoon I'd scheduled for pie? "Perhaps I'll actually write that book review," I thought, "or grade a few more papers."

I wanted to make pie.

Curried Apple and Mushroom

Why did I want to make pie? Because I wanted to be productive. Pie was a *product*—tangible, sensory—of my creativity, something to show for my effort. I also thought I might write an essay, but that takes months, years. Pie can be done in a few hours. I could grade papers, but there's no satisfaction there. I wanted something to mold with my hands.

Writing, grading, cooking: these are the things I think to do when bored. Things not on that list: making the bed, putting in another load of laundry, mopping the floor, mowing the lawn. All things Kirsten would rather I did than make pie. I suppose in this way, I'm guilty of being that man who supports women in the workplace but still expects them to do the chores. So many conversations start with Kirsten saying, "I know you cleaned the kitchen, and I'm grateful, but there's more to the house than that." Then she worries about filling that horrible stereotype of the nag, and I feel guilty for needing the reminder, ever the absent-minded and slovenly husband. We're uncomfortable with these roles, but keep playing them out, the weakness of one edging up against the insecurity of the other.

When we started Pie Month, we worried we would grow bored with pie, that we would fill up on desserts, or that hurried crusts with lame fillings would be our norm. When I say *we*, I really mean Kirsten, who was understandably wary of the experiment from the beginning. I, ever enthusiastic, was confident I could make something gourmet every time.

I felt I'd failed when Kirsten lost interest.

As I write this, Kirsten worries that this essay makes her appear unsupportive, the kill-joy to my boundless enthusiasm. And I worry that I should put my energy into something lasting, or at least helpful, concerned my passions don't matter, that my silly whims are forced on her.

Maple Pumpkin with Walnuts

Doubt about my enthusiasm isn't new; we almost broke up over it.

We sat in the dark on the concrete steps of my duplex. Kirsten explained where she felt our relationship wasn't enough. There were many small things, but they all came down to her feeling like I cared too much, just not for her. She asked why I couldn't be as enthusiastic for her as I was about my other interests: squirrels, essays, obscure holidays. She asked why all I ever did was invite her over for meals.

I told her: "You're the only one I ever cook for. Maybe I'll get better at it, but this is how I say I care for you."

Our worries continue: I keep cooking. She enjoys it, and I enjoy it, but we both know it isn't everything.

Caramel Apple

One of our running jokes from when we were dating is that Kirsten and I will tell each other, "I love you like _____." The first expression was "I love you like pizza" because, for reasons I don't quite remember, I yelled this out the window as a pizza delivery man drove by. But, because of our love for pastries, this morphed into "I love you like butter." When we lived in Kazakhstan, far from the ocean, we said *sushi*. When Kirsten makes her caramel apple pie, I say *pie*.

"The pie makes you love me?" she asked. "Does it make you want to make love to me?"

"Yes," I replied, "but before we eat it; afterward, I'll be too full."

Salted Caramel Banana Freezer Pie

The most difficult part of foreplay became not knowing where it would lead. After kissing, caressing, moving our hands over each other, I'd feel aroused, have all the same sensations I had when I'd been healthy, but there would be no physical manifestation. I imagine it may have been something like the experience of amputees with phantom limbs.

Those tender preludes to sex, always pleasurable whether coy or brash, were now fraught, uncertain, unproductive. Whether I or Kirsten pulled away first, embarrassed for having tried, I felt ashamed for not living up to the task. If she reassured me that it was fine, I knew she was feeling generous; if she silently rolled over and tucked herself deeper into the covers, I knew she thought it was her, as though she'd done something wrong. Some nights, I would press my body against hers by way of apology; some nights I turned too, and we slept back-to-back.

Pie Shakes

Pie was an important part of our courtship. We frequented Sammy's for pie shakes, a milkshake with a slice of pie dumped in. Also, the first Pi Day after we met, Kirsten told me she was going to make a pie for the Pie Party I was hosting. I didn't have high expectations for her pie. Not that I thought she was a bad cook, but she seemed skeptical of the Pie Party idea and only announced that she'd decided to make a pie at the last minute. Plus her sister was visiting, so I figured they had other ways to occupy themselves.

She appeared with a raspberry and cream pie with a large Π baked across the top. It was easily the most beautiful pie at the event and one of the most delicious.

I had made an asparagus potpie that oozed green roux and sat uneaten.

This was not the first time Kirsten surprised me with her baking skills. Our first date was to an art exhibit and lecture about bees as enjoyable as it was brief. Anxious to prolong the evening, I suggested we get a dessert with honey in it. "I can make baklava," she said.

So we drove to the store, and she picked out the phyllo dough, nuts, and honey. At my place, she showed me how to lay out the dough a few sheets at a time, brushing on the butter and then the nut-sugar mixture, layer after layer, pouring the honey glaze after it had all been assembled. It would be months before she realized how sexy that was, but that night we stayed up way too late, chatting on the concrete steps outside my duplex, the porch light shining down on us.

Shepherd's Pie

Concerned about my manhood, I begin taking precautions, all pulled from Internet sites or common sense developed from no experience whatsoever. I already walked two miles to work, but I walked faster to increase my circulation. I stopped crossing my legs when sitting. I drank more water. I snacked on nuts and dark chocolate. I researched herbal remedies and bought a mix called "Male Power," guaranteed to get my libido up and which I thought of as the "sex pills," the same joking name I previously had for Kirsten's birth control, though she hadn't taken that since we returned from Kazakhstan. When my pills arrived, I kept them hidden in my desk. But after only a few days, I was more ashamed of hiding them than what they meant, so I put them in the same place she kept her pre-natal vitamins.

Bean and Cheese Empanadas

The night of the empanadas, I told a coworker about Pie Month. It was a chatroom meeting for my online job, so I couldn't read her facial expressions, but she seemed impressed.

"How fun," she wrote. "Your wife must really be taking care of you."

Had we been in-person, the silence would have been awkward.

I explained that I was the one making the pies. The lady seemed surprised to learn that a man could cook. Or maybe she was amazed that a man *would* cook. Perhaps it's unfair of me to think so, but when a woman expresses surprise about my cooking, I assume her husband is unhelpful around the house, just sits on the couch watching sports while the babies cry. Really, I fear this about myself, that all I do is clean up my own kitchen messes.

A few days later, Kirsten posted a picture on Facebook of the fish tacos I made for dinner, and a friend said, "I'm jealous. Of your dinner. Not your husband. Unless he cooked it alone."

Perhaps it's conceited of me to say so, but the "alone" is comical. I didn't grow up to expect a man not to cook. I learned as much about the kitchen from my father as from my mother, and my brothers and sisters are equally capable with a skillet. My little brother baked a tableful of cakes for our wedding reception, most of them from Julia Child's *Mastering the Art of French Cooking*.

I often prided myself when people made such comments. But then again—though I was teaching at two universities, trying to write more, trying to keep up with grading, doing most of the reading for my classes, occasionally taking out the trash without being asked, and never feeling keen about the lines society draws for household duties—when people expressed surprise about finding me in the kitchen, I was just as likely to think they were really saying, "Shouldn't you be doing something else right now?"

Lemon Meringue

We wanted chickens. Ostensibly, they were for the humanely sourced eggs, but there was some nostalgia there, too. Kirsten had hens as a child, and I, having successfully cultivated zucchini in ages passed, considered myself something of an urban homesteader.

During Pie Month, we were still in the planning stages: Kirsten researched how to build a coop.

I investigated which breeds lay colorful eggs.

Frito Pie

When we moved to West Texas, we visited the gynecologist together. It was almost seven months since Kirsten's emergency surgery in Kazakhstan, where doctors who did not speak our language removed a fist-sized tumor from her uterus. One nurse told Kirsten she would never have children. Countless others told her to stop crying. Our surgeon said everything would be fine. Six months and we'd be good to go.

The American gynecologist didn't even ask to look at the scar, but Kirsten insisted. The doctor poked it and smiled approvingly. She asked a few questions about how Kirsten was feeling—fine, no more pain. The doctor said we were free to start trying for children. As we left, she said, "Have fun."

Little Debbie Snack Pies

We decided we wanted children on I-70, just east of the Colorado border, where the hills are green in late summer and the Rockies' full height purples the horizon. We were driving to visit her parents, our engagement still recent. We talked about waiting a few years, but not too many. We talked numbers: just two or three children, despite both coming from typically large Mormon families. We knew we'd feel pressure to have more.

"We'll take them one at a time," I said.

We didn't talk about why we wanted kids. For both of us, it was a natural desire. But even then, before we knew there would be issues, before we knew about the surgery, about my impotence, Kirsten was practical enough to ask: "What if we can't have kids?"

We talked about that again as the difficulties arose, with childlessness becoming a foreseeable future. But the condition was so recent, adoption bureaucracy so thick, our time in Texas so impermanent.

"It'll pass," she assured me.

Mushroom Quiche

After a lazy Sunday afternoon nap, I woke to the smell of sautéing onions and mushrooms. Buttery crust.

"It was really easy," Kirsten said. "I'd make this again." She told me she even improvised, something I don't see her do much. "We didn't have dry mustard, so I used turmeric."

Six carefully placed spinach leaves broiled on the top. She hadn't mentioned the conception app in over a week.

Apple Cheddar

The internet ads were the worst part. Because of my Google searches and the "sex pill" purchase, the sidebars pictured men in striped boxers sitting on the edges of beds, faces buried in hands, women in white negligees looking rejected or sympathetically sad behind them. I saw myself over and over in the click-bait: always wounded or wounding Kirsten.

"I know," I wanted to say. "Don't show me the problem. Offer solutions."

Pear and Pesto Pizza

One chilly morning, we built a garden bed. We measured and marked an outline with string and sticks, then built a gray brick bed in the spindly grass. We did the math together, calculating the cubic feet of dirt we'd need to fill the bed.

I learned to build gardens when I was young, one of the few handy skills I picked up from my father. As the seventh child, I came into the world when my parents were already established, when they'd already become suburban. We moved a few times, always into newer houses. The bare yards needed landscaping. With my father's guidance, I made dirt lots into something you'd want to look at. While I'm clueless with wires, screws, or hammers, I can, with some confidence, stack landscape bricks. I can lay sod and build paths through it. I can make the tomatoes fruit and the mint spread.

Even so, despite double-checking, we underestimated by more than half the amount of soil we needed. I made three trips to the store to haul enough dirt.

Angel Pie with Custard and Mixed Fruit

Besides not eating from the fruit of the tree in the garden, the only other commandment Adam and Eve had was to multiply and replenish the earth. Tend the garden. Make babies. Be fruitful. Don't eat that fruit.

Many traditions teach that had they not fallen, we'd be walking in the garden with God, not toiling for bread.

Mormons don't see it that way. If Eve hadn't eaten the fruit, if Adam hadn't followed her, the two of them, ignorant of pain and progress, would have remained childless. The two commandments were contradictory: Either stay, innocent and naïve, or leave and populate the world. Eve chose, breaking one rule to follow a higher. Adam followed, knowing Eve couldn't do it alone. The temple presentation also teaches that the Fall necessitated Christ's condescension, making it something to celebrate.

"But why give contradictory commandments, then?" Kirsten asked, as has anyone who's thought about the story for more than a few minutes.

There are lots of Sunday school answers but no satisfying ones. I do know this: God let Eve make her own choices, even when she didn't know anything.

The Veggiepottomus Artisanal Pizza

Maybe a more relevant question was what the contradiction meant for us. What were we to choose? What do we choose when having children seemed not to be a choice?

Eve chose wisdom.

Adam chose Eve.

Pecan Pie with Cinnamon Swirl Crust

This one we made together. Kirsten rolled out the crust, sprinkled cinnamon, pressed the pinwheels to the plate, carefully arranged every twist. When we're cooking together, Kirsten does the technically difficult detail work. I made the filling, going heavy on pecans and spices. Kirsten placed each nut individually in a spiral on the top.

Everyone Liked this pie on Facebook. People were impressed by the crust. People asked for the recipe. But it wasn't worth the hype. We've made better. But you don't share those parts on Facebook; you just pass the links around and pretend everything is how you want it.

Fresh Berries with Cream and Custard

Kirsten's book club asked if she was getting tired of pie. She said yes, and told me so later, as we stood before the freezer door, too sugar-sick to eat a whole slice, just taking a spoonful each to say we'd done it.

With a bit of guilt in her voice, she said, "Pie used to be a treat."

Welsh Pasties

My grandma Morris—a Southern belle—learned to make pasties from her Welsh mother-in-law. It's peasant food: ground beef, potatoes, onions, salt, a pat of butter in simple crust. My great-great-grandfathers took it with them into the quarries. As a child, I helped my grandma fill the pasties after she prepared the dough. Grandma served the pasty with a cabbage relish she called "corn pickle," a recipe I've improved on, adding garlic and bell peppers to the corn, cabbage, and onions.

Someday, I hope, I will have children and grandchildren to teach this recipe to. We'll eat it for family gatherings, for birthdays and wedding lunches, for graduations and extended visits. And when they ask me how to make the crust, I will say what my grandma told me: "It's just like pie crust, but you add less shortening."

Sweet Potato Hand-pies

Sometimes, Kirsten asked, "What do you think is wrong?" and sometimes she just said, "Don't worry." Though I did worry, about everything: being a father and husband, writing papers, planning lessons, putting pie on the table. Would Kirsten think my lackluster performance meant I wasn't attracted to her? She told me she worried about that, too, that with her work making her more stressed, being a little depressed, her weight going up—all that pie—she wouldn't be surprised if I didn't like her any more.

"Lots of men have these sorts of problems," I said, mostly to reassure her that it was just physical. I knew attraction wasn't the issue. But not knowing what the real issue was, I doubted my own conviction even there. Perhaps I was actually gay and not bisexual, but even that I hadn't told her about yet. Perhaps we weren't in love. I pushed away those toxic thoughts. They were irrational.

"I know," she said, snuggling close, the sheets pulled up to hide our nakedness. "It's just a little speed bump."

She meant it in all seriousness, to reassure me, but I started laughing at the words *little* and *bump* and couldn't stop.

Rocky Road Mousse

The last day of Pie Month, and neither of us wanted pie. Purely to say we did it, we each took a bite, obligatorily nibbling the chocolate, marshmallows, and pecans.

Though we felt glutted from too much dessert, we looked at Pie Month and called it good. We had conquered it together.

Still, it was hard to feel entirely pleased with ourselves as we stood in our kitchen, the windows out to the garden black. Kirsten's job was busier and harder; she wanted to quit. She came home crying most nights. She wanted to be the one to make dinner but didn't want to take that away from me. My semester was winding up, getting busier and busier as it always did. We hungered for good news to share. More full than satisfied, we returned the pie to the freezer and went to bed.

OF SAINTS AND SEEDS

Just yesterday, though the yard is still dusted with snow, Kirsten and I planted seeds in tiny germination pots and gave them the sunniest spot in our house, which has caused the cat some distress, as she had previously claimed that corner for herself. Squash, herbs, and leek seeds now wait for spring, and we wait for them. We have walled off a garden plot in the front yard, but I feel the grittiness of the dirt and the biting wind and doubt anything will ever come of this. But in the back of my mind, I remember that first garden, the one I had in college. How improbable of a gardener I was, yet how it bloomed.

SOON AFTER I MOVED INTO a duplex with friends, I immediately asked if I could use the backyard—just a weed lot and some parking spaces—to plant vegetables, not because I had any experience with gardening, but because I liked the idea of it. The landlord said yes, and I started digging. My friends helped with the groundbreaking and we pulled the tall grasses up, reveling in the rich soil. In a few hours, we cleared a ten-by-ten-foot space. We dug holes, planted seeds; dirt got under our fingernails, in our hair, and across our cheeks, leaving us itchy, sneezing, and pleasantly muddied.

WHEN ONE CONSIDERS A GARDEN—whether fresh tilled dirt with seeds yet to germinate, or in the height of production, or a plot of sun-withered vines—it is easy to believe in pagan deities of fertility and death. It is no wonder that early philosophers explained the miracle of agriculture through the supernatural. Living green slowly bursting out of moist blackness: the most potent of magics. How else could life sprout from the ground and then wither as suddenly, if not for gods caught in a cycle of feuds and divine whims?

Gods of Nature, because they are invisible and stuck in a rut, seem as plausible as any modern explanation: no matter how far down we see into the seed we can imagine a level further. Perhaps, once we uncover the innermost core of every seed, we will see the God in Charge of Spring hunched over on a minuscule throne, weaving vines like yarn. Despite my inclination for science, I like this image and don't know that it is far off.

If I were Catholic, I might get some explanation of the wonders of growth from the Patron Saint of Gardeners, whom most people think is Saint Frances of Assisi because statues of Assisi with cute little squirrels, deer, and birds are frequently found in gardens. But, it's actually a lesser-known guy named Saint Fiacre, a gardener from Ireland who moved to France sometime in the mid-600s AD. Maybe it's him inside every seed, not on a throne, but working a minuscule garden while he whistles a tune, his sleeves rolled up to reveal his sunburned arms plucking weeds like hymns from the soil.

OF ALL THE WEEDING TO BE DONE—and there is always plenty—the lettuce and spinach required the most work, mostly because in my amateur enthusiasm I planted the seeds too close together. Leafy greens sprouted up in a dense row. I had to move slowly, unwinding the spinach and lettuce from each other and then from the weeds. If I moved too quickly, I would ultimately pull up the vegetables with the weeds or leave the plants injured. I filled my iPod with Simon and Garfunkel albums, enjoying the slowness of a morning listening to good music and weeding.

One day, I was sitting on the ground giving my fingers a workout as I carefully rifled through the spinach. I got about halfway down the first row, music filling my ears—

April, come she will,
When streams are ripe and filled with rain.

—when I saw something moving. I jumped back quickly. It was thin and wriggling, a smoky burgundy. A snake, I thought.

As the creature progressed out of the middle of my salad greens, I saw that it was not a snake but an earthworm. No garden-variety earthworm, though: it was at least a foot long. It slithered quite effortlessly—faster and smoother than I would have thought a worm could go—toward Hamlet, the decorative horse skull that resided in my garden.

I was hoping the worm would crawl into the skull, because that would have been a gruesome, Shakespearean image, but instead, it slipped behind a small leaf and disappeared. I lifted the leaf and saw no signs that a worm of any proportion had been there. He must have reentered the earth without slowing. That such a thing could happen—that a worm could move so quickly and yet jerkily, disappear without even a trace of its path—I never before would have imagined. This was a sign that forces I could never understand were at work in this garden, and that this garden, though I had planted it, was not solely my domain.

There were plenty of other creatures who made their home in my plot. Lots of insects: several ant colonies thrived at various times and in various locations, and with each new hill, I retaliated by shoving mint sprigs down the hole, infuriating the residents; slugs loved the cabbages; and potato bugs lived in the damp darkness under my mulch. An escaped luau pig once took refuge there until, in trying to catch it, my roommates and I chased it out, leading to a neighborhood chase that involved the police—who had no idea what to do with a loose pig—until the unlucky pig was wrestled into submission by the hosts of the luau. I like to think that the quiet moments in the garden were the pig's last peaceful moments on earth. Several dogs made the garden part of their regular rotation through the neighborhood, exploring with their noses a ground that seemed forever new. Our neighbor's kittens learned to hunt in the garden, chasing grasshoppers and stalking the low-hanging blades of cornstalks.

Also, the quail. The mama and the babies explored the garden every morning, pecking around and looking for whatever it is that quail eat while the papa sat on the telephone wires overhead, watching. When a stranger (me, for example) got too close, the papa sounded the alarm and the family escaped to the bushes near the fence. I stalked them further, trying to get a closer look, but they hid in the branches, so all I could see was a bush trembling as though it burned.

I WASN'T RAISED WITH PATRON SAINTS, but I appreciate the tradition, especially regarding Fiacre. Having a good friend who loved gardening as much as I did would have been nice, one who understood the vegetal allure and who thrilled at the smell of crushed mint. If that friend happened to be chummy with the God of Zucchini Sprouting, so much the better. It never occurred to me to pay homage to Fiacre, but it's nice to think that he might have actually cared about my garden, might have had some influence on the soil and the health of the seeds. As a Mormon, I had been raised to follow the God Who Delights in Gardens—a god who started the world in a garden and began his own sacrifice in another—but is still difficult to believe that, with so much else a god probably attends to, he would have spent much time in my garden. On the other hand, a patron saint, especially a lesser-known one, might have more time to attend to such duties. Fiacre would have had his choice of the world's most splendid gardens, but I like to imagine him keen on the humbler patches. As I see it, our exchange would have happened something like this:

I am working in the garden, down on my knees begging the shoots to come out, digging my bare hands into the dust to pull out the weeds, thorns, and thistles as sweat slowly drips down my face. Then I hear whistling, and, looking up, I see Fiacre coming around the side of the house, his wide-brim hat flopping, his sandaled feet hitting heavily against the driveway's asphalt, his gray robes enveloping him like morning fog. I smile and wave, then wipe the moisture off my brow. Fiacre carries a spade in one hand and a boom box in the other. He places the boom box next to us, produces a tape from his large gray sleeves, and inserts it into the machine. Music sways over us:

I'd rather feel the earth beneath my feet
Yes I would...

Then he kicks off his sandals, rolls up his baggy sleeves, and joins me in the garden.

I never expected him to help often, though, because Fiacre, my friend, is a busy man: patron saint of taxi drivers, box makers, sufferers of venereal diseases and hemorrhoids, tile makers, florists, hosiers, barren women, pewterers, and plowboys. A care-laden man, he doesn't have much time for the mundane work of gardening any more. But I think he visited anyhow, in the early morning hours when the stars were only just fading, with no one to disturb the sound of silence in my secluded patch of vegetables. He sat there, as mesmerized as I was by the crisp, herby smells, flicking little blessings on the garden.

BUT EVEN FIACRE'S BLESSINGS don't stick to everything; he's no easy-miracle saint.

The cantaloupe vines flourished all summer, the flowers delicate and lovely, the leaves vibrant and green, the fruit large and fragrant. When I went to pick the ripe fruit, I found maggots.

I planted the watermelon in the same place the following summer. A few small fruits grew, but they never matured. There was one that looked like it was going to succeed, but my brother accidentally stepped on it.

The garden store sold me a packet of kholrabi seeds, and I was excited to try what I thought would be an exotic vegetable. The seeds had been mixed up and only radishes grew.

It took three tries to succeed at oregano. The first attempt was from seed, and it never sprouted at all. Then I bought a plant from the hardware store, and it died a few days later. Near the end of the first summer, at a farmers market, I came across a woman behind a wide table spread with herbs and flowers and was immediately attracted to her oregano. I would like to say there was a heavenly light, or a still small voice, or that she spoke with the rushing of winds. But it was nothing like that; the woman sat in the shade of her tent, minding her potted herbs and her frolicking children with equal ease as she answered questions from her camp-chair cathedra.

I was intrigued by the oregano, since I had been defeated before, and asked her if this was a hearty variety. She said that it was. Nothing I could do would kill it. It would last me many years.

It didn't take long to kill it.

First, I stepped on it and broke all the stems off. Then, I dragged the hose violently across it, trampling it further. It got flattened even more during a Guy Fawkes Day bonfire. The sticks went dry and brittle, and the few leaves left withered away. Well before the winter snows came, I gave up all hope for it. But one day, while I tended the spring garden so many months later, I looked over at the spot where the oregano had been. Curious, I began snooping around the weeds, hoping there would be maybe one small sprig. I didn't see anything, but when I was done, I smelled oregano on my hands. I crouched down on my knees for a closer look. I crushed and smelled each leaf; then I found it, not just a sprig, but a bush of oregano at least four inches tall and across. I cleared away the weeds and watered the resurrected plant amid a complete lack of angelic singing.

PART OF MY NOSTALGIA FOR that college garden is that I have had no luck with gardening since. After this first garden, which thrived so well for two summers, I lived for many years in apartments without land to cultivate. Though I did try gardening in pots the very next summer, it was without success. After getting married, our basement apartment was completely surrounded by black asphalt. Then, we moved to the wintry land of Kazakhstan, where we lived sixteen stories up and didn't even know the names of the vegetables we ate. Here in Texas, we've built a garden bed and filled it with the best soil. I watered and weeded as diligently as I had before, but still, it is land I am unfamiliar with, and the sun is harsher than I am accustomed to, the wind strange. In three summers, we've gotten a few zucchinis, one or two mealy tomatoes, but nothing else for three summers in a row.

Even the seedlings we planted so early in the season are struggling: the cat, probably out of revenge, has taken to eating down the pea shoots. We'll be lucky if any remain to be planted.

I FREQUENTLY SAW MY ROOMMATES or the people who lived in the duplex's other apartment snooping around the garden, or walking up and down the rows as they talked on their phones. The first year, we had a pair of neighborhood children sneak into our backyard frequently; they asked if they could have one of the pumpkins for their Jack-o'-lantern, and I was happy to give it to them, just as I was happy to give away zucchini, lettuce, peas, and tomatoes to anyone who even looked in the garden's direction.

My most memorable visitor came one morning during the first summer; it must have been around six, when the morning was just lighting up behind the mountains. When I woke, I looked outside, surprised to see a strange man. He seemed like a man of many worries, momentarily detached from them all as he breathed in the garden air through a cigarette. In the early light, everything about him was gray: his shaggy hair, his shirt, his jeans, his halo of smoke. He sat on a cinder block against the dry, graying wooden fence, flicking a butt into the corn. Among the vibrant greens of the garden, he looked like a weed, by which I mean that he looked as though he belonged but had come without my bidding. I wanted to take a picture of him, but I dressed and got outside only in time to see him duck into my neighbor's gray sports car.

In my imagination, I whirled around just in time to catch one last glimpse of the gray man as he gathered up his spade and boombox, tucked his cloak under him, and ducked his head into my neighbor's car, now a taxi. Instead of hearing heavy metal, before the *crump* of the door sealed us from each other, I heard the opening strains of "Sound of Silence."

Hello darkness, my old friend…

IN MANY OF THE SUNDAY SCHOOL lessons I heard on the subject of faith, the teacher used planting seeds as an analogy: The gardener shows her faith by planting seeds, knowing that by watering, pruning, weeding, and nurturing, she will reap what she has sown and thus confirm her faith in the seeds, and the soil, and nature, and, of course, the God of the Harvest, a god who rewards those who labor. Until I was a gardener myself, I was satisfied with this analogy and was inspired by the planter's competence. Even distanced as I am now from faith, I still like the analogy overall, but what it doesn't cover is that a gardener like myself so often didn't deserve the harvest. I trampled my herbs; I crowded the greens too close together; I left the melons too long on the vine; I over-watered the peppers; I let irreverent strangers help and they crushed the watermelon and pulled up the cilantro, thinking it was sweet-smelling weeds. But even when I watered, pruned, weeded, and nurtured correctly, the garden suffered the whims of nature: the ants ate the mint seeds before they spouted; the tomatoes caught the many diseases they are prone to; worms and slugs ate the fruit when it was ripe; and for no reason that I could detect, an otherwise healthy plant only produced one cucumber all season.

And yet, the corn was sweet. The peas strained and popped as I bit them. The radishes were the largest, reddest, crunchiest radishes. I ate my fill of tomatoes fresh off the vine and still had enough for nights of red dinners. The zucchini produced so many of its long fruit that they rotted on my counter before I could eat them all, and I told my roommates that they needed to eat more squash, and they said they couldn't eat it any more frequently than every meal, and before the vegetables on the counter were gone, I was carrying more armfuls into the house, and making loaves and loaves of zucchini bread. This was not my miracle to claim. No, I've never had enough faith to produce such miracles, to feed a multitude from seven packets of seed and a few potted sprouts. Perhaps there is a God of Abundance, perhaps there is not, but I have seen reasons enough for reverence in the presence of anything green.

XENOMANCY

Would you believe in love at first sight?
Yes, I'm certain it happens all the time.

—Lennon and McCartney

When I first drove into Lubbock, the sky and trees, the roads and roofs were all one vintage photograph: shades of dull green, mostly brown, everything covered in fine dust. I felt queasy. I hadn't wanted to move to Lubbock, but Texas Tech was the only school that had offered me a stipend, and we didn't want to risk debt just for a more charming location. But the view wasn't doing much by way of first impressions. Furthermore, I only knew one person in Lubbock—Bruce, a man I'd worked with years before—a strange fellow who had recently posted on Facebook: "Lubbock finally has a Panda Express!"

"At least we'll have Panda Express!" Kirsten and I had mocked as we planned our move from Kazakhstan back to the US. In many ways, the Lubbock landscape was the same that we'd just left on the Steppes: flat, wind-blown, and dirty around the edges. We had approached Kazakhstan with the eyes of foreigners, had seen in our first sights of Astana's eccentric architecture an adventure unfolding, but a year later, back in the States, I was not awed by the rundown homes on the side of Lubbock's freeway. I passed the Panda Express as I took the Marsha Sharp Freeway into town, passing the university, looking for my exit to our one-bedroom, one-month lease. We'd been back in the States for less than a week. Kirsten was in Utah getting our things out of storage, and I'd come straight here after a family reunion in California. My orientation started the next day, and I pulled into town hungry, tired, and unsure about all this dust.

I unloaded my suitcases and an air mattress from the car, my hopes for the evening resting on the one other contact I had in Lubbock, though we'd not actually met in person. Mike was another soon-to-be graduate student in the English department, and we'd connected via Facebook. I had noticed from his profile that, like me, he sported a reddish beard, loved good food, and was Mormon, so a friendship seemed inevitable. We'd shared some emails back and forth, and he invited me to dinner the night I arrived in town.

At his house, his wife, Hilary, served *caldo verde*, a Portuguese soup with pureed potatoes, *linguiça* sausage, and greens. They had moved in several weeks prior, from San Antonio, but Mike had family history in Lubbock as recently as his father's childhood, and that put me at ease a little. This was a place like any other. Their toddler son ran naked through the small duplex, hugging my legs. The friendship seemed fast fixing.

After my orientation meetings, I flew to Denver to meet Kirsten at her parents' house, loading more things into our moving truck. The next day, I drove into Lubbock for the second time in a week. I pointed out the Panda Express as we passed it. We laughed earnestly, but Kirsten cried just a little. We immediately started planning our getaway: an early graduation, epic road trips, a semester in a Spanish-speaking country.

Mike came to our apartment that night, dropping off a large bowl of pasta salad with lots of vegetables, fresh bread, and homemade jam. Kirsten felt ragged, and our apartment was a mess of boxes, so I met Mike at his car instead of inviting him up. But as Kirsten and I ate, sitting on the floor with flattened boxes as our table, our patio furniture overturned and stacked in the living room, we talked.

"It's so nice of them," Kirsten said. "They don't even know us."

"Plus, it's excellent that they gave us vegetables," I said, feeling the weight of car food.

As we considered the bread and jam, the pasta with vegetables, I recognized the signs of a friendship forming and remembered the lesson we'd learned in Kazakhstan: you can make any place livable with friends. For the first time since deciding to come here, we felt like Lubbock could be home.

THAT MIKE AND HILARY COULD become friends so quickly, so easily, with so little known about either of us, is a sort of miracle, but a miracle I've experienced often enough to expect it. For example, in eighth grade, we were told in Sunday School that a new boy would be joining our class soon. When I arrived at the mid-week activity, I saw Grant in the room and knew before we'd spoken that we'd be friends immediately—something about his smile, the way he looked up when I entered. Likewise, in college, I noticed Logan in my dorm's hall and cafeteria, and I told my roommate that we needed to get to know him because we'd be friends. Logan is as close as a brother now. Perhaps this is my superpower, xenomancy: the ability to tell the future by observing strangers. For someone like me who is more comfortable alone and often awkwardly aware of my own nerdiness, xenomancy allows me to bypass certain social graces, jump right into assuming we are friends when I get the itch, as when I approached Joel the first day he moved into our congregation and said "Do you like board games? Because if you do, we're going to be great friends." Of course, he did like board games, and of course we are great friends, as my superpower had alerted.

But such a power is not always put to use. In social gatherings, I am reserved, unconvinced anything I might add to a conversation will be interesting. At conferences and other professional minglings, I feel like an interloper. If there is a party, I will find my way to the kitchen and offer my help, where I am free of small-talk responsibilities and able to occupy my hands. Even in normal day-to-day circumstances, I must continually convince myself that my professors, coworkers, fellow congregants find me tolerable. Instead of asking help from people I am convinced would do it only as professional obligation, I cultivate an unhealthy self-discipline and solitary work ethic. The fact of the matter is I'm comfortable in the relationships I have and rather greedy with my personal time. Even when I sense that someone might be a great friend, it doesn't always seem worth the energy required to transmute strangers into friends, even when there is a catalyst of shared religious background, a new move, the willingness to share a meal. Mike and Hilary were happy exceptions, perhaps because we and they were both new to town and our social circles so sparse.

In a world with so many choices, the smallest inconvenience can result in conscientious decisions not to befriend someone, to think them not worth the time. Just recently, some three years after making our home in Lubbock, I was in Cuenca, Ecuador—our dreams of a Spanish-speaking semester realized thanks to online teaching appointments and student loans—and I saw a couple on the opposite curb of a busy street. Something about her knee-length cut offs and his stubbly beard, the pace of their gait, the ease of their smiles, their youthful faces (we young gringos were the odd-ones out there in retirement paradise); I knew we could be friends. I could have waved them down and asked what they were doing in South America and heard a story similar to our own: wanderlust, novelty, liberal education. The world is everywhere whispering friendships, but I was happy in my isolated, aimless walks through a city where I was *extranjero*, stranger, a word which implies more than the English because it comes from *extrañar*, which is both "to estrange" and "to miss." It implies desire; it acknowledges that the traveler in strange places has some other place they may be longing for, belong to. Someone longing for them. Maybe it doesn't do all that for native speakers, but I love my interpretation.

Which is all to say I rationalized seeing those gringos on the street as just an omen for a good walk. We were only there for a few months, then back to Lubbock. Too much trouble and energy to befriend someone out of the blue. We didn't need the friends, had already made several in the short time we'd been in Cuenca. This was not one of those times when I needed new friends, had been on the lookout for them, like as an undergraduate, when you long for it, need others, don't "have a life" without friends to stay up with. The need is so deep, you could have gone up to practically anyone in the library, introduced yourself, and received an invitation to a party that night. You could meet your soulmate with just a little innocent flirting. Anything was possible.

But I didn't feel that urgency on the street in Cuenca, nor the wider sense of possibility. I've got my soulmate; I've already cemented lifelong friendships. Of course, I recognize that there is room for surprise, but when Kirsten and I returned to Lubbock to take exams and write dissertations, we returned to a place we reluctantly call home, not to a city whose people we don't know. We returned to friendships already solidified. Here, we can give excellent restaurant recommendations for any occasion. We no longer fear the dust storms, but instead make sure the windows are closed tight and then watch with a certain pleasure as the air grows gritty, the sunlight diffuses into a pink-yellow haze, and the friction electrifies the whole city.

WHEN WE WERE YOUNG, we asked "What if?" with a certain amount of actual potential. *If* was a dare, not nostalgia. But looking back, "What if?" becomes a scarier question. Kirsten and I ask it sometimes about ourselves. Not, "What if we hadn't met?" but "What if we'd met earlier?"

After we started dating, we discovered that years before we had attended the same party, hosted by our one mutual friend, Liann. I didn't know many people at the party, and, not one to invite small talk with strangers, I spent the whole night in the kitchen with Liann making crepes which were then sent out to the guests. Kirsten swears she came into the kitchen at some point to talk with Liann, but we don't have any memory of meeting each other. We sometimes ask, What if we'd actually met then? What if we'd had the same chemistry that we had when we met years later?

We're both glad there was no immediate connection. Neither of us was particularly pleased with who we were at the time, neither of us quite as mature as we'd hoped to be. Had there been a spark of attraction, it probably would have fizzled out because I hadn't wanted a real relationship, would have pushed her away at the first sign of trouble.

IN THE END, IT WAS KIRSTEN who saw me, who experienced what you might call "love at first sight," but Kirsten just tells people I was her "insta-crush," and that she didn't expect anything to come of it. We both attended a new congregation on the same day and happened to sit next to each other in Sunday School. (Or so I had thought; Kirsten told me much later she had intentionally sat next to me after crushing on me from a distance.) We talked about my starting a master's program that month, about her teaching at an alternative high school. She and her roommates talked about me when they got home from church. I didn't even remember her name, but when I learned it the next week, I mistook her for my freshman roommate's sister, because they are both Kirsten Anderson.

"I know your older brother!" I said excitedly, without checking, despite "Anderson" being a very common last name and Kirsten's last name being spelled with an *e*. (How was I to know that?)

"Who, James?" she said. "Cameron?"

"No, Aaron."

"I don't have a brother named Aaron."

"Oh."

And so it went: flirtatious glances, a few dates, and then we were married, living in Lubbock by way of Kazakhstan, going for late night runs to Panda Express, with a baby on the way.

AND BABIES ARE THE STRANGEST sort of strangers. Strangers you intentionally invite into your home and who you are required to love at first sight. You stock up the house, but you can't prepare for them. Or know them. Until suddenly, they arrive and re-focus the entire quality of the house.

Both times Kirsten and I drove home from the ultrasound lab I heard Michael Bublé's "Just Haven't Met You Yet" on the radio, the lyrics: "Wherever you are, whenever it's right, you'll come out of nowhere and into my life." And, as the song says, together, we'll be so amazing. Which I knew was true because of the way our in-utero child moved their hand over their face. Because of the slope of their toes, the serenity of the brow. Hard to say just what binds you to a person you don't even know, when all the knowledge you have is from a wave of a hand gesture and a grainy picture. Obviously, there were also biological forces at work here: studies have shown that a father's hormones fluctuate during pregnancy, too, though far more subtly than a mother's dramatic physiological changes. Men and women alike, we are wired to love our offspring, and maybe that is a miracle, too, its own sort of superpower. I'm not claiming that the love and concern I automatically felt for this child in utero are somehow unique or that my quality of love is somehow superior. It is, I expect, rather common, but even though I expected this love, anticipated this connection, I was surprised by it, amazed how a bond formed so effortlessly just by seeing via ultrasound the child's hand covering its face.

KIRSTEN AND I DIDN'T WANT to know the sex of our child until birth. Perhaps Kirsten was just humoring me, but I felt like I needed to meet the child as they were, without pretense. Our parents weren't thrilled; they wanted to be efficient in choosing appropriately gendered clothing for the newest grandchild, as though we needed anything besides gender-neutral onesies with squirrels. Even strangers seemed to disagree with our choice to wait; "Of course you'll learn the sex for the *next* child" a woman in the waiting room told me while we waited for a check-up. But for me, not knowing was the only way. We had a list of names for either gender, couldn't even narrow it down to one for each. How could you know what to name a person you've never met? I wanted time to think of my child as a person first, as someone who I got to meet like you do most others: face first. Kirsten's cousin, pregnant at the same time as us, said she felt much more connected to the fetus once she knew she was carrying a daughter, but I think I would have been disappointed with the certainty of anything. I wanted my child to be a person first, a tangible presence, and everything else later.

So, when Kirsten woke me at one a.m. saying she thought her water broke, I didn't feel too worried about anything, though we hadn't even packed a hospital bag yet. Here came a stranger who wouldn't be a stranger much longer. I tried to have no expectations so that the surprise of it, the joy of it, could come to the forefront.

"Well," I said, putting on trousers and throwing a sweater over my head, "let's go meet our kid."

When we turned out of our neighborhood onto the normally busy but now deserted Indiana Ave, we saw a gray fox crossing the street, and I recognized a good omen.

SHORTLY AFTER KIRSTEN JOINED ME in Lubbock, and after some of the boxes were unpacked and school had started, after Mike and I learned we'd randomly been assigned as office mates, when we were feeling just a little more settled, Mike and Hilary invited Kirsten and I over for dinner.

As we pulled out of our apartment's parking lot and approached the underpass at Marsha Sharp and Slide, Kirsten said she was nervous.

"We don't know these people," she said, "but we're going to their house for dinner."

"But in a year, five years, they'll be our best friends."

"I know," she said. "That's why I'm anxious."

And we were right, or seem to be. When they were expecting their next child and we were in Ecuador, we mailed them a Panda Express gift card because Hilary was too nauseous to cook, and well before that, they were the first to bring us a meal after the obstetrician pulled from Kirsten's cesarean-opened belly our son, purple and wrinkled, who we named Cal after the character in *East of Eden*, a reminder that each person has potential. As the nurse held him and he turned to us, his skin turning pink, his lungs filling for the first time, I recognized all the signs: his hands curled together, then unfurled themselves as his mouth opened in a wide pink gasp.

<<<<>>>>

AUTHOR'S NOTE

I began writing the first essay in this collection, "Nothing in Particular," almost 20 years ago, when I was a much different person than I am today. I remember the night I began writing particularly well: I worked at Brigham Young University's Creative Works Office, and in the evenings after the real adults went home my fellow undergraduates and I would browse Facebook in our cubicles, watch movies in the conference room, and hang together in a space that felt like our own little secret. I started writing "Nothing in Particular" at my desk in the receptionists' area during one of those after-hour get-togethers. My nonfiction workshop class was expecting an essay draft in the morning, but I'd not yet started. In a moment of cheeky, anxious honesty, and mostly just in the hope that something would happen, I started to write: "I have nothing to write about." Then, I just kept going, at first as a joke and then as an idea I became fully invested in.

At the time—new as I was to the essay form, still thinking it a mere side quest in my goal of being a science fiction novelist—I would have told anyone that I thought the best essays, or at least *my* best essays, were a bit cheeky and honest, grasping for Truth. What I wouldn't have told anyone was the actual truth. I carefully edited the details of my inner life, little-white-lied, and skirted around any subject that took my essays anywhere near certain confessions:

that despite being very active in my faith, I had significant religious doubts, and that, as church pamphlets put it, I "had same sex attraction." While writing and editing the first drafts of this collection, I presented the front of a devout, straight man.

When I finally had the courage to come out, my former professor and now friend Pat Madden wondered if he had missed something in what I'd written during those years, and I replied that he hadn't: every essay I'd written had been carefully crafted to omit the truths I didn't yet feel safe enough to own. That terrible irony haunted me: Essays should be a genre about vulnerability and honesty, but in all of my own writings, I had lied.

I could have stayed in the closet a long time: Bisexuality is often called the "invisible sexuality," and mine certainly was. I am a rather vanilla cis-gendered man in a monogamous partnership with a cis-gendered woman; no one suspects much. But it was my conviction in the essay that finally gave me the courage to free myself from the closet. I wanted to write the essay that is now "A Study in Comfort," at the heart of which is the moment I realized I loved Kirsten precisely because of her open support for queer people, a rarity in our conservative circle. I started writing that essay before I'd even come out to Kirsten, though we'd been married almost a decade by then. Which is to say, I was honest in an essay long before I was ever honest with the people in my life, even the person who is most dear to me. Only the act of essaying, of sitting for a while in discomfort and reaching toward new understandings, gave me the nerve to say so what I actually felt inside.

I wanted this book to reflect who I really was, but starting over would have meant writing a book entirely different than this one was trying to be. Instead, where appropriate, I've edited the essays to mention my sexuality. I suspect some readers might notice that discussions of my sexuality and my desires are stained by a religious anxiousness born from teachings that my thoughts were unholy and damnable. I no longer believe I need to repent for being attracted to men, but for a long time I did and these essays reflect that worry. Perhaps some readers will take this anxiousness to be an anti-queer stance or even just less than enthusiastically proud. I hope they will see instead that these essays are trying, at last, to be honest.

Scott Russell Sanders has written that essays "better speak from a region pretty close to the heart," and I hope more people will find the safety to do so. I hope anyone reading this will know, as I now do, that you don't have to be afraid of your own heart. I'm also happy to report that my next project, Magpie Zines, is unapologetically queer.

ACKNOWLEDGMENTS

These essays owe a lot to the editors and readers who accepted the original versions into various journals and anthologies.

Several essays previously appeared in journals and anthologies: "Of Complicated Themes" in *SLAB Journal*, "Trains in the Night" in *Wanderlust: A Narrative Map*, "Points of Tangency" in *Proximity Magazine*, "The Common Area" and "My Library" in *Superstition Review*, "Speak English, Please" in *The Chattahoochee Review*, "If We Had Been Allowed the Take Pictures" in *Brevity*, "Of Saints and Seeds" in *Remembered Arts Journal*, and "Pie Month" in *Revising Eternity* (University of Illinois Press). This last one, I also owe a large thank you to the editor, Holly Welker, whose careful editing made that essay so much better than when it started.

Though all of the essays were edited for continuity and clarity from their original versions, the following were especially changed from their originally published versions, almost to the point of new essays: "Nothing In Particular" in *Prick of the Spindle*, "On Whom Things Are Lost" in *Blue Lyra Review*, "I Thought of You" originally published as "Memento Sciurus" in *Stone Voices*, and "Lives Yet to Be Lived" originally published as "Looking for Squirrels: A Love Note" in *WILDNESS Journal*.

Several of the essays in this collection began as drafts in writing workshops, specifically from my wonderful professors Patrick Madden, Jacqueline Kolosov, and Leslie Jill Patterson, all of whom have become so much more than teachers to me, but mentors and exemplars of terrific human beings.

Much of this book was re-written and revised when I lived in South Korea. Special thanks goes to my then-employer, The University of Utah Asia Campus, for its generous provision of resources to support faculty development. While there, I was also part of the Incheon Writers Collective. These essays and my creative journey would not be what they are today without the thoughtful criticism and earnest friendship from this international group of creatives.

Thank you to Dr. Ross Tangedal and Cornerstone Press for finding value in this collection. Eva Nielsen, Ellie Atkinson, and Chloe Cieszynski were excellent editors to work with. Allison Lange designed the perfect cover for this book. Thank you, also, to Ava Willett for social media assistance and Sophie McPherson for sales and events.

And, of course, Kirsten, who I have more to thank for than I can adequately express here: for her permission to include her in the pages of this book, for being the first person to make me feel safe, for critical and loving editing of my work, and for being a true partner. I love you like butter.

Scott Russell Morris is a writer and enthusiast. He's a mixed-media artist, zinester, and a board gamer. He is a native of California now living in Iowa, where he is an Associate Professor of English and Creative Writing at Cornell College. He is the creator and editor of Magpie Zines.

You can find him online at www.skoticus.com